THE BOOK OF CRICKET LISTS

'I HOPE THIS BOOK
IS A BIG HIT FOR YOU'

From Jonty
xxx.

D0892465

THE BOOK OF CRICKET LISTS

introduction by **Tom Graveney OBE**
edited by **Norman Giller**
with an opening spell by **Eric Morecambe OBE**

Futura

A *Futura* Book

Copyright © 1984 Norman Giller

First published in Great Britain in 1984
by Sidgwick & Jackson Ltd, London

This edition published in 1985
by Futura Publications, a Division of
Macdonald & Co (Publishers) Ltd
London & Sydney

ISBN 0 7088 2782 9

Printed and bound in Great Britain by
William Collins, Glasgow

Futura Publications
A Division of
Macdonald & Co (Publishers) Ltd
Maxwell House
74 Worship Street
London EC2A 2EN
A BPCC plc Company

I dedicate this book to the memory of my good friend Eric Morecambe, who in his role as Past President of the Lord Taverners provided an entertaining opening spell shortly before the sad end of his great innings in 1984.

Rest easy, Eric, and thanks for bringing us all the sunshine of your smile.

NORMAN GILLER

CONTENTS

OPENING SPELL by Eric Morecambe OBE   17

INTRODUCTION by Tom Graveney OBE   19

SECTION ONE: The Greatest by the Greatest

Sir Len Hutton's 10 Greatest Opening Batsmen   21
Michael Holding's 10 Greatest West Indian Fast
  Bowlers   22
David Gower's 10 Greatest Left-Handed Batsmen   23
Mike Brearley's 10 Greatest Slip Catchers   25
Godfrey Evans's 10 Greatest Wicket-Keepers   26
Alec Bedser's 10 Greatest Medium-Pace Bowlers   27
Fred Trueman's 10 Greatest Fast Bowlers   29
Jim Laker's 10 Greatest Spin Bowlers   30
Barry Norman's Dream Team   31
Derek Randall's 10 Greatest Fielders   32
Basil D'Oliveira's 10 Greatest Battlers   34
Ted Dexter's 10 Greatest Stroke Players   35
Lance Gibbs's 10 Greatest Spin Bowlers   37
Colin Milburn's 10 Greatest Entertainers   38
John Arlott's Dream Team   39
Brian Statham's 10 Greatest New Ball Partners   41
Farokh Engineer's 10 Greatest Wicket-Keepers   42
Bobby Simpson's 10 Greatest Slip Catchers   43
John Lever's 10 Greatest Left-Arm Fast Bowlers   45
Derek underwood's 10 Greatest Left-Arm Spin
  Bowlers   46
Eric Sykes's Dream Team   47
Bishop David Sheppard's 10 Greatest Batsmen   48
Colin Cowdrey's 10 Greatest Test Grounds   50

Bob Taylor's 10 Greatest Wicket-Keepers 51
Ray Lindwall's 10 Greatest Fast Bowlers 52

SECTION TWO: Heroes of the Heroes

Dennis Amiss 54
Trevor Bailey 55
Alec Bedser 56
Ian Botham 57
Brian Close 59
Denis Compton 60
Colin Cowdrey 62
Willie Rushton's Dream Team 63
Mike Denness 64
Ted Dexter 65
Bill Edrich 66
Bobby Moore's Dream Team 67
John Edrich 69
Godfrey Evans 70
Keith Fletcher 71
Mike Gatting 72
Sunil Gavaskar 74
Graham Gooch 75
David Gower 77
Tom Graveney 78
Kim Hughes 80
Sir Len Hutton 81
Ray Illingworth 83
Trevor Howard's Dream Team 84
Imran Khan 86
Syed Kirmani 87
Michael Bentine's Dream Team 89
Alan Knott 90
Jim Laker 91
David Larter 92
John Lever 94
Tony Lewis 95
Dennis Lillee 97

Rodney Marsh   98
Leslie Crowther's Dream Team   99
Peter May   100
Colin Milburn   102
Derek Shackleton   103
Francis Matthews' Dream Team   105
Reg Simpson   106
Mike Smith   107
John Snow   109
Brian Statham   110
David Steele   112
Brian Johnston's Dream Team   113
Bob Taylor   114
Fred Titmus   116
Fred Trueman   117
Derek Underwood   119
Frank Bruno's Dream Team   120
Dilip Vengsarkar   121
Peter Walker   122
Doug Walters   124
Wasim Bari   125
Bob Willis   126
Jimmy Greaves's Dream Team   128
Bob Woolmer   129

SECTION THREE: Finest of the Finest

Dennis Amiss, Geof Arnold Trevor Bailey   131
Alec Bedser, Ian Botham   132
Geoff Boycott, Mike Brearley, David Brown, Tom
    Cartwright   133
Brian Close, Denis Compton, Colin Cowdrey,
    Mike Denness   134
Ted Dexter, Bill Edrich, John Edrich   135
Godfrey Evans, Keith Fletcher, Mike Gatting   136
Sunil Gavaskar, Graham Gooch, David Gower   137
Tom Graveney, Kim Hughes, Sir Len Hutton   138
Ray Illingworth, Imran Khan, Doug Insole   139

Syed Kirmani, Alan Knott, Jim Laker   140
David Larter, John Lever, Tony Lewis   141
Dennis Lillee, David Lloyd, Brian Luckhurst,
    Rodney Marsh   142
Peter May, Colin Milburn, Arthur Milton, Arthur
    McIntyre,   143
John Murray, Alan Oakman, Jim Parks, Pat
    Pocock   144
John Price, Peter Richardson, Brian Rose, Derek
    Shackleton   145
Phil Sharpe, Reg Simpson, Alan Smith, Mike
    Smith, John Snow   146
Brian Statham, Dick Spooner, David Steele, Roy
    Tattersall, Bob Taylor   147
Fred Titmus, Roger Tolchard, Fred Trueman   148
Derek Underwood, Dilip Vengsarkar, Peter
    Walker, Doug Walters   149
Johnny Wardle, Wasim Bari, Allan Watkins, Peter
    Willey   150
Bob Willis, Don Wilson, Bob Woolmer, Doug
    Wright   151

SECTION FOUR: Best of the Rest

BATTING:
Dennis Amiss, Bob Barber, Ian Botham   152
Geoff Boycott, Mike Brearley, Brian Close, Denis
    Compton   153
Colin Cowdrey, Mike Denness, Ted Dexter, Bill
    Edrich   154
John Edrich, Keith Fletcher, Mike Gatting   155
Sunil Gavaskar, Graham Gooch, David Gower,
    Tom Graveney   156
Kim Hughes, Sir Len Hutton, Imran Khan   157
Syed Kirmani, Tony Lewis, Brian Luckhurst, Peter
    May   158
Colin Milburn, Arthur Milton, Brian Rose, Phil
    Sharpe, Mike Smith, David Steele   159

Dilip Vengsarkar, Peter Walker, Doug Walters,
  Allan Watkins   160
Bob Wyatt, Norman Yardley   161

Patrick Moore's Dream Team   162

BOWLING:
David Allen, Geoff Arnold, Trevor Bailey, Jack
  Birkenshaw   163
Alec Bedser, Bill Bowes, David Brown, Tom
  Cartwright   164
Godfrey Evans, Alf Gover, Ray Illingworth,
  Robin Jackman   165
Alan Knott, Jim Laker, David Larter, John Lever,
  Dennis Lillee   166
Rodney Marsh, Arthur McIntyre, John Murray,
  Jim Parks   167
Pat Pocock, John Price, Mike Selvey, Derek
  Shackleton, Alan Smith   168
John Snow, Brian Statham, Roy Tattersall, Fred
  Titmus   169
Roger Tolchard, Fred Trueman, Derek
  Underwood, Bill Voce, Johnny Wardle   170
Bob Willis, Don Wilson, Doug Wright   171

SECTION FIVE: The Sporsmen's Sportsmen

David Allen, Dennis Amiss, Geoff Arnold, Trevor
  Bailey   172
Bob Barber, Alec Bedser, Ian Botham, Geoff
  Boycott, David Brown, Tom Cartwright   173
Brian Close, Denis Compton, Colin Cowdrey,
  Mike Denness, Ted Dexter, Bill Edrich, John
  Edrich   174
Godfrey Evans, Keith Fletcher, Sunil Gavaskar,
  Graham Gooch, David Gower   175
Tom Graveney, Kim Hughes, Sir Len Hutton, Ray
  Illingworth, Imran Khan, Doug Insole   176

Syed Kirmani, Robin Jackman, Alan Knott, Jim
  Laker, David Larter, John Lever   177
Tony Lewis, Dennis Lillee, David Lloyd, Brian
  Luckhurst, Rodney Marsh, Peter May, Colin
  Milburn, Arthur Milton   178
Arthur McIntyre, John Murray, Alan Oakman,
  Jim Parks, Pat Pocock, John Price   179
Peter Richardson, Brian Rose, Derek Shackleton,
  Phil Sharpe, Reg Simpson, Alan Smith   180
Mike Smith, John Snow, Brian Statham, Dick
  Spooner, Roy Tattersall, Bob Taylor   181
Fred Titmus, Roger Tolchard, Fred Trueman,
  Derek Underwood, Dilip Vengsarkar, Bill
  Voce, Peter Walker   182
Doug Walters, Johnny Wardle, Wasim Bari, Allan
  Watkins, Bob Willis   183
Don Wilson, Bob Woolmer, Norman Yardley   184

SECTION SIX: Around the Grounds

Dennis Amiss, Geoff Arnold, Trevor Bailey, Alec
  Bedser, Geoffrey Boycott   185
Mike Brearley, David Brown, Tom Cartwright,
  Brian Close, Denis Compton, Mike Denness,
  Ted Dexter, Bill Edrich   186
John Edrich, Godfrey Evans, Keith Fletcher, Mike
  Gatting, Sunil Gavaskar, Graham Gooch, David
  Gower   187
Tom Graveney, Kim Hughes, Sir Len Hutton, Ray
  Illingworth, Imran Khan, Doug Insole   188
Robin Jackman, Syed Kirmani, Alan Knott, Jim
  Laker, David Larter, John Lever, Tony Lewis,
  Dennis Lillee   189
David Lloyd, Brian Luckhurst, Rodney Marsh,
  Peter May, Colin Milburn, Arthur Milton,
  Arthur McIntyre   190
John Murray, Alan Oakman, Jim Parks, Pat
  Pocock, John Price, Peter Richardson, Brian
  Rose   191

Derek Shackleton, Phil Sharpe, Reg Simpson,
   Alan Smith, Mike Smith, John Snow, Brian
   Statham   192
Dick Spooner, David Steele, Roy Tattersall, Bob
   Taylor, Fred Titmus, Roger Tolchard, Fred
   Trueman, Derek Underwood   193
Dilip Vengsarkar, Bill Voce, Peter Walker, Doug
   Walters, Johnny Wardle, Wasim Bari, Allan
   Watkins   194
Peter Willey, Bob Willis, Don Wilson, Bob
   Woolmer, Doug Wright   195

SECTION SEVEN: For Argument's Sake

All-star Star-Sign Teams:
Capricorn/Aquarius   196
Pisces/Aries   197
Taurus/Gemini   198
Cancer/Leo   199
Virgo/Libra   200
Scorpio/Sagittarius   201
A Team of Left-Handers   201
The Bespectacled Brigade   201
Foreign-Born England Test Players   202
Cricketing Footballers   202
A Team of All-Rounders   203
Commenting Cricketers   203
County Select:
Derbyshire/Essex/Glamorgan/Gloucestershire   204
Hampshire/Kent/Lancashire/Leicestershire   205
Middlesex/Northamptonshir/Nottinghamshire/
   Somerset   206
Surrey/Sussex/Warwickshire/Worcestershire   207
Yorkshire   208
A Team of Post-War Test Captains   209
International Post-War All-Stars   209
Ernie Wise's Dream Team   210
Dream Match 1: Fathers v Sons   211

Dream Match 2: Older Brothers v Younger
  Brothers   211
Dream Match 3: World Pre-War X1 v World Post-
  War X1   212
Dream Match 4: England v Rest of the World   212
Tim Rice's Dream Team   213

SECTION EIGHT: TOP TEN TABLES
compiled by Malcolm Rowley

The Batting Masters   214
The Bowling Kings   217
Nicholas Parsons' Dream Team   220
Top Individual Test Scores   221
Top Wicket-Takers in a Test Match Innings   221
Top Ten Test Wicket-Keepers   222
Top Ten Test Catchers   222
Top Ten Career Aggregates (Batting)   223
Top Ten Career Aggregates (Bowling)   223

ACKNOWLEDGEMENTS

I wish to thank the compilers of the following books which were top of my list for reference checks:

Wisden Cricketers' Almanack, the 'Bible' of the game; *The Complete Who's Who of Test Cricketers* by Christopher Martin-Jenkins; *The Wisden Book of Test Cricket* by statistical wizard Bill Frindall; Roy Webber's 1952 *Who's Who in World Cricket;* various *Playfair Cricket Annuals*; the magnificent *Barclay's World of Cricket* edited by E.W. Swanton and John Woodcock; James Gibb's *Test Cricket Records; The Cricketers' Who's Who* edited by Iain Sproat; also various issues of *The Cricketer* and *Wisden Cricket Monthly*, two marvellously informative magazines.

In particular I would like to thank all the cricketers and celebrities who willingly answered my irritating questions, some of them originally for *Cricket Heroes* – a one-off magazine that I published in conjunction with Lord's Taverners. Not one of them asked for a penny piece in return for their time and information. On their behalf I am making a donation to the Lord's Taverners, the famous charitable organisation that does so much to support youth cricket and to help the handicapped and less fortunate of this world.

My thanks also to batting master Tom Graveney for bringing the voice of authority to this book and to Roy Ullyett, cartoonist genius of the Daily Express, for his Eric Morecambe caricature.

NORMAN GILLER

Note: The date given against each individual entry refers to the player's first-class career span.

OPENING SPELL
ERIC MORECAMBE OBE
Past President of the Lord's Taverners

It gives me great pleasure. It always has and, touch wood of the willow, it always will. I'm talking about cricket, of course. The game is in my roots. I can trace my ancestry back to the great W. G. Grace. Well, almost. My Auntie Grace was an outstanding all-rounder with the Billington and District Brass Band XI. You should have seen her googlies. She was dropped after whipping out the bandleader's middle stump with a long hop. Not a pretty sight!

But I digress. I've been handed the new ball and asked to bowl the opening spell in this *Book of Cricket Lists*. A lot of my heroes are among the contributors and Tom Gravy, who poured himself into many great performances for England in Test matches, has added his considerable authority to a book packed with fascinating lists compiled by some of the finest cricketers in the world. It was always my ambition to play in a Test for England. There was just one problem. I was allergic to grass. A pity because I would have been the silliest mid-on ever to have played Test cricket. My long leg would have been a sensation and there have never been swingers to match mine. I used to be such a magnificent fielder that they composed a piece of music as a tribute. It's called the Third Man Theme.

The idea for this *Book of Cricket Lists* was hatched during my third year as President of the Lord's Taverners, a marvellous charity organisation that helps to provide minibuses for handicapped children and to support and maintain adventure playgrounds. Norman Giller, the orchestrator of the book, whom I have known and avoided for many years, has made a generous donation to the Taverners in return for the co-operation of all the famous contributors. If you are interested in becoming a friend of the Taverners you can get all the information you need by writing to The Director, Lord's Taverners, 1 St James's Street, London SW1A 1EF.

If you're a cricket lover you will find that once you've picked up this book it will be very difficult to put down. That could have something to do with the chewing-gum substance that the publishers have worked into the cover but, more likely, because of the absorbing facts and opinions that you will find in the following pages.

Before handing over to the one and only Tom Gravy – coming in to bat at the Taverners' end – I have just one question to ask: 'Be honest now, folks . . . what d'you think of it so far . . .?'

ERIC MORECAMBE

18

INTRODUCTION
TOM GRAVENEY OBE

How on earth do you follow that unique man of comedy Eric Morecambe? With great difficulty! Anyway, I am delighted to introduce a book that will provoke many debates and discussions among cricket lovers who will all have their own ideas and opinions as to which players should be listed in the many different categories.

The line-up of contributors to this *Book of Cricket Lists* reads like a Who's Who of Test cricket. Just to give you an idea of their quality here are two teams that I have selected from among the 85 post-war stars featured in the following pages:

ENGLAND	REST OF THE WORLD
Len Hutton	Sunil Gavaskar
Geoff Boycott	Bobby Simpson
Peter May	Dilip Vengsarkar
Denis Compton	Kim Hughes
David Gower	Imran Khan
Ian Botham	Farokh Engineer
Godfrey Evans	Ray Lindwall
Jim Laker	Rodney Marsh
Fred Trueman	Dennis Lillee
Derek Underwood	Michael Holding
Bob Willis	Lance Gibbs

In Section One – The Greatest by the Greatest – I have given personal assessments of each of the contributors, all of whom have produced performances on the cricket field that well merit them being labelled 'The Greatest'. While it is very much a book of opinions, editor Norman Giller has also provided 'For the Record' facts and figures to help settle any arguments, with a final section by statistician Malcolm Rowley providing tell-tale 'Top Ten' tables that reveal the most prolific run makers and wicket takers in Test match history.

As well as the expert opinions of the Test players, there are also entertaining contributions from an array of cricket-loving celebrities who have made 'dream team' selections. The star selectors are, in batting order: Barry Norman, John Arlott, Eric Sykes, Willie Rushton, Bobby Moore, Trevor Howard, Michael Bentine, Leslie Crowther, Francis Matthews, Brian Johnston, Frank Bruno, Jimmy Greaves, Patrick Moore, Ernie Wise, Tim Rice and Nicholas Parsons.

Now it's over to you for the great selecting game . . .

TOM GRAVENEY

SECTION ONE
THE GREATEST BY THE GREATEST

Top ten ratings by the giants of cricket

SIR LEN HUTTON'S
TEN GREATEST OPENING BATSMEN

 1 **JACK HOBBS** *(England, 1905–34)*
 2 **BARRY RICHARDS** *(South Africa, 1964–   )*
 3 **HERBERT SUTCLIFFE** *(England, 1919–45)*
 4 **ARTHUR MORRIS** *(Australia, 1940–55)*
 5 **SUNIL GAVASKAR** *(India, 1966–   )*
 6 **CYRIL WASHBROOK** *(England, 1933–59)*
 7 **GLENN TURNER** *(New Zealand, 1964–   )*
 8 **GEOFF BOYCOTT** *(England, 1962–   )*
 9 **GORDON GREENIDGE** *(West Indies, 1970–   )*
10 **ANDREW SANDHAM** *(England, 1911–37)*

'The easy part was selecting Jack Hobbs as No. 1 on my list. The hard part was deciding the other nine because I had to leave out so many oustanding opening batsmen. Hobbs and Sutcliffe were the perfect opening partners. They could play on all types of wickets and were excellent judges of a run. Barry Richards was a fine strokemaker of the highest class and the player I would hold up as an example for any young schoolboy to try to emulate.'

SIR LEN HUTTON

TOM GRAVENEY: 'If I were making a list of openers, there is no doubt that Len Hutton would be my opening choice. The main job of any opener is to lay the foundation for an innings and it was a job Len did better than anybody else. The fact that he averaged 56.67 in his 79 Test matches provides all the evidence that is necessary to prove his remarkable consistency.'

MICHAEL HOLDING'S
TEN GREATEST WEST INDIAN FAST BOWLERS

1 **WES HALL** *(Barbados, Trindad and Queensland)*
2 **ANDY ROBERTS** *(Leeward I., Hants and Leicestershire)*
3 **ROY GILCHRIST** *(Jamaica)*
4 **CHARLIE GRIFFITH** *(Barbados)*
5 **JOEL GARNER** *(Barbados and Somerset)*
6 **COLIN CROFT** *(Guyana and Lancashire)*
7 **KEITH BOYCE** *(Barbados and Essex)*
8 **MALCOLM MARSHALL** *(Barbados and Hampshire)*
9 **VANBURN HOLDER** *(Barbados and Worcestershire)*
10 **UTON DOWE** *(Jamaica)*

'I have only listed players that I have either seen or have had first-hand information about, rather than digging too far back into the past. Wes Hall was a player whose performances inspired me when I was a youngster just learning about the game. He had a classical action and a sporting but competitive nature. His partnership with Charlie Griffith used to cause an explosion of interest and excitement in the West Indies when I was a schoolboy and I used to dream of one day bowling just like them in Test cricket. Uton Dowe is perhaps the least well known outside the West Indies but he was popular in Jamaica where, though sometimes erratic, he could really whip the ball down.'

MICHAEL HOLDING

22

TOM GRAVENEY: 'Michael Holding would come close to the top in most lists of the world's all-time greatest fast bowlers. He reminds me very much of his boyhood hero, Wes Hall. He has a beautiful action and is good to watch provided you're not the batsman waiting to receive balls that are bowled as quickly as any in the history of the game. His approach to the wicket is smooth and graceful and umpires have told me they cannot hear him running in, so light is he on his feet. He can get life and lift out of the most docile wicket.'

FOR THE RECORD

Michael Holding was born in Kingston, Jamaica on 16 February 1954. A university graduate, he started his first-class career with Jamaica in 1972 and joined Lancashire in 1981 after starring in Lancashire League cricket with Rishton. His most impressive bowling performance was against England in the 1976 Test at The Oval. There was no pace in the wicket yet he managed to generate tremendous speed and claimed 14 wickets for 149 runs in one of the greatest spells of sustained fast bowling ever witnessed. In the same 1976 series, in which he established himself as a giant of the game, he took five for 17 in 14.5 overs at Old Trafford to rush England out for 71 on a treacherous pitch.

DAVID GOWER'S
TEN GREATEST LEFT-HANDED BATSMEN

1 **GRAEME POLLOCK** (*South Africa, 1960– *)
2 **SIR GARFIELD SOBERS** (*West Indies, 1953–74*)
3 **ALVIN KALLICHARRAN** (*West Indies, 1966– *)
4 **CLIVE LLOYD** (*West Indies, 1963– *)
5 **JOHN EDRICH** (*England, 1959–78*)
6 **ROY FREDERICKS** (*West Indies, 1963–77*)

7 **ALLAN BORDER** *(Australia, 1976–   )*
8 **LARRY GOMES** *(West Indies, 1971–   )*
9 **DAVID HOOKES** *(Australia, 1975–   )*
10 **DAVID LLOYD** *(England, 1965–   )*

'It would have been easy to include such masters as Neil Harvey and Frank Woolley, but impossible to make a personal judgement on any order of merit. Thus I have settled for a list of ten left-handed "greats" from recent years whom I have at least seen play.'

DAVID GOWER

TOM GRAVENEY: For sheer elegance and artistry, there are few batsmen around today – left- or right-handed – to compare with David Gower. He has great natural talent and has added discipline and concentration to his game in recent years to make himself the *complete* batsman. David's mention of Neil Harvey fills me with nostalgia. I would bracket him with Garfield Sobers and Graeme Pollock as the finest left-handed batsman I played against.

FOR THE RECORD

David Gower was born in Tunbridge Wells on 1 April 1957 and started his first-class career with Leicestershire in 1975. He was elected Young Cricketer of the Year in 1978 by the Cricket Writers' Club and revealed his staying power with an unbeaten 200 for England against India at Edgbaston in 1979. After a series of inconsistent performances he was left out of the Test squad but re-established himself as one of England's most exciting and gifted batsmen during the 1981 tour of the West Indies. A brilliant fielder, he gave up studying law to concentrate full-time on cricket. He was appointed Leicestershire captain in 1983 and succedded Bob Willis as England skipper.

MIKE BREARLEY'S
TEN GREATEST SLIP CATCHERS

1 **BOB SIMPSON** *(Australia, 1952–78)*
2 **PHIL SHARPE** *(England, 1958–76)*
3 **GRAHAM ROOPE** *(England, 1964–   )*
4 **TONY GREIG** *(England, 1965–80)*
5 **GREG CHAPPELL** *(Australia, 1966–   )*
6 **WALLY HAMMOND** *(England, 1920–51)*
7 **ROLAND BUTCHER** *(England, 1974–   )*
8 **IAN BOTHAM** *(England, 1974–   )*
9 **MIKE HENDRICK** *(England, 1969–   )*
10 **CLIVE LLOYD** *(West Indies, 1963–   )*

'Briefly, the reasons for my selections – Simpson and Sharpe because they were both brilliant at slip to slow or quick bowlers; Roope, Greig and Chappell because of reflexes that made them magnificent slip fielders to fast bowlers; Hammond as a concession to the pre-1960 era; Butcher, Botham and Hendrick, less reliable than the first six but all capable of absolutely stunning catches; Lloyd, a late arrival at slip – an extremely safe pair of hands and with an incomparable reach.'

MIKE BREARLEY

TOM GRAVENEY: 'A wicket-keeper in his early days, Mike developed into an outstanding first slip capable of snapping up the half chance. The great concentration he gave to his captaincy did not rob him of the ability to put his mind to fielding and his catching was an inspiration to his team-mates. Walter Hammond and Bobby Simpson were the greatest slip fielders I ever saw, with Colin Cowdrey, Mike Brearley, Tony Greig and Keith Miller just a fingertip behind them.'

FOR THE RECORD

Mike Brearley was born at Harrow, Middlesex, on 28 April 1942. An intellectual, he was respected as one of the most perceptive and intelligent tacticians in modern cricket. In his four years as a Cambridge Blue (1961–64) he amassed what remains a university record haul of 4,348 runs. He became Middlesex captain in 1971 and succeeded Tony Greig as England skipper. There have been few to match him for being able to motivate the players around him. He had a good calculating cricket brain and knew how to get the best out of his team in every situation.

GODFREY EVANS'S
TEN GREATEST WICKET-KEEPERS

1 **DON TALLON** *(Australia, 1933–54)*
2 **RODNEY MARSH** *(Australia, 1968–   )*
   ALAN KNOTT *(England, 1964–   )*
   BOB TAYLOR *(England, 1960–   )*
5 **FAROKH ENGINEER** *(India, 1958–76)*
6 **JOHN MURRAY** *(England, 1952–75)*
7 **JOHN WAITE** *(South Africa, 1948–65)*
8 **WALLY GROUT** *(Australia, 1946–66)*
9 **WASIM BARI** *(Pakistan, 1966–   )*
   SYED KIRMANI *(India, 1967–   )*
   DERYCK MURRAY *(West Indies, 1960–   )*

'As you will be able to deduce from my list, I found it agonisingly difficult to settle on a final selection. Players of the calibre of Don Brennan, Gil Langley and Clyde Walcott kept tugging at my memory but their Test experience behind the stumps was fairly limited. I am preparing a book on the 'Great Wicket-Keepers of the World' and will be able to name 50 or more whom I have admired over the years. Getting that list down to ten was, I found, an impossible job!'

GODFREY EVANS

TOM GRAVENEY: 'For sheer exuberance, enthusiasm and match-winning brilliance, 'Godders' was a one-off. They threw away the mould when they made him. He was acrobatic, extremely agile and he kept all his team-mates on their toes with his competitive drive and good humour. He was, for me, the tops as a wicket-keeper.'

FOR THE RECORD

Godfrey Evans was born in Finchley, Middlesex, on 18 August 1920. His first-class career with Kent spanned 20 years from 1939 to 1959. In 91 Tests, he held on to 173 catches and made 46 stumpings. He was England's first-choice wicket-keeper between 1946 and 1959. Only his Kent successor Alan Knott and Rodney Marsh have claimed more victims in Test cricket. An accomplished batsman, he scored more than 1,000 runs in a season four times and scored seven centuries including two in Test matches. His total dismissals were 1,060 – 811 caught and 249 stumped.

ALEC BEDSER'S
TEN GREATEST MEDIUM-PACE BOWLERS

1 **SYDNEY BARNES** *(England, 1894–1930)*
2 **MAURICE TATE** *(England, 1912–37)*
3 **HUGH TRUMBLE** *(Australia, 1887–1903)*
4 **GARFIELD SOBERS** *(West Indies, 1953–74)*
5 **BILL JOHNSTON** *(Australia, 1945–54)*
6 **AMAR SINGH** *(India, 1931–40)*

7 **CHARLIE TURNER** *(Australia, 1882–87)*
8 **FAZAL MAHMOOD** *(Parkistan, 1943–63)*
9 **GEORGE LOHMANN** *(England, 1884–97)*
10 **IAN BOTHAM** *(England, 1974–   )*

'These are not in any particular order of merit because obviously I did not have the good fortune to see the old timers in my list play. But conversations with great past masters such as Sir Jack Hobbs gave me respect for their ability. I had the privilege of playing in a charity match with Amar Singh in 1937 and he lived up to all I had heard about him. He could swing and cut the ball and had devilish pace off the pitch. As Wally Hammond once remarked, "He came off the pitch like the crack of doom."

ALEC BEDSER

TOM GRAVENEY: 'English cricket has not had a better servant than Alec Bedser. His main bowling weapon was an in-swinger that continually had batsmen in difficulties but his deadliest delivery was a leg-cutter that moved like a fast leg-break. Added to the penetration of these wicked deliveries, Alec had exceptional line and length, great control and the biggest heart in cricket.'

FOR THE RECORD

Alec Bedser was born at Reading, Berkshire, on 4 July 1918. Playing for Surrey from 1939 until 1960, he took 1,924 wickets at an average 20.41. He claimed 236 wickets in 51 Tests for England. His best bowling analysis was eight for 18 for Surrey against Notts at The Oval in 1952. He gave a carbon copy performance the following season, taking eight for 18 against Warwickshire. Alec was a key member of the Surrey team that won seven successive County championships. He has been a leading administrator since 1962. His identical twin, Eric, was also a first-rate cricketer with Surrey.

FRED TRUEMAN'S
TEN GREATEST FAST BOWLERS

1 **RAY LINDWALL** *(Australia, 1945–60)*
2 **KEITH MILLER** *(Australia, 1937–59)*
3 **BRIAN STATHAM** *(England, 1950–68)*
4 **LES JACKSON** *(England, 1947–63)*
5 **WES HALL** *(West Indies, 1955–71)*
6 **ALAN DAVIDSON** *(Australia, 1949–63)*
7 **GRAHAM McKENZIE** *(Australia, 1959–75)*
8 **DENNIS LILLEE** *(Australia, 1969–   )*
9 **RICHARD HADLEE** *(New Zealand, 1971–   )*
10 **ANDY ROBERTS** *(West Indies, 1970–   )*

'All these great bowlers had the common denominator of being able to deliver the unplayable ball on all wickets and at the highest possible level. I have stuck to fast bowlers of post-war years. If I had started dipping back into the past I would have got caught up with marvellous pacemen like Harold Larwood and Bill Voce. Compiling this list was hard enough as it was!'

FRED TRUEMAN

TOM GRAVENEY: 'Fred Trueman was (and is) a great character who had the heart of a lion and was a master of self-motivation. He was expert at making the ball leave the bat with away swing and seam and was an aggressive, totally committed competitor. His 307 Test wickets are lasting evidence of his effectiveness. It's interesting to see Les Jackson, the old Derby warhorse, included in his list. Les was desperately unlucky to get only two England caps. He could be virtually unplayable when bowling flat out on those notorious green 'uns in Derbyshire.'

FOR THE RECORD

Frederick Sewards Trueman was born at Stainton, Yorkshire, on

February 1931. At the tail end of his career (1949–69) he briefly played for Derbyshire but it is with his beloved Yorkshire that he will always be associated. He took 2,304 wickets (average 18.29) during his career, including what was a world record 307 in 67 Tests. Taking 100 or more wickets in ten successive seasons, he had his most prolific year in 1960 with 175 victims at an average 13.98 runs. He took ten or more wickets in a match 25 times and completed four hat-tricks. Fred is now a respected radio commentator and a hard-hitting cricket columnist with the *Sunday People*.

JIM LAKER'S
TEN GREATEST SPIN BOWLERS

1 **BISHEN BEDI** *(India, 1961–82)*
2 **RICHIE BENAUD** *(Australia, 1948–64)*
3 **BRUCE DOOLAND** *(Australia, 1945–57)*
4 **LANCE GIBBS** *(West Indies, 1953–76)*
5 **CLARRIE GRIMMETT** *(Australia, 1911–40)*
6 **BILL O'REILLY** *(Australia, 1927–46)*
7 **HUGH TAYFIELD** *(South Africa, 1945–62)*
8 **WILFRED RHODES** *(England, 1898–1930)*
9 **DEREK UNDERWOOD** *(England, 1963–   )*
10 **HEDLEY VERITY** *(England, 1930–39)*

'I have made my selection in strictly alphabetical order as the task is difficult enough without any further classification! If you are going to judge them on wickets taken, then Wilfred Rhodes has an untouchable record. This colossus of Yorkshire cricket claimed 4,187 victims at an average 16.71 runs in an extraordinary 32-year career. He could turn the ball on any surface but it was his subtle variations of flight that bemused most batsmen.'

JIM LAKER

TOM GRAVENEY: 'Jim's 19 wickets for 90 runs in the 1956 Old Trafford Test against the Australians will stand for all time as a statistical monument to his genius. He was the greatest off-spinner of them all. He had a model action, could make the ball turn sharply and was always deadly accurate.'

FOR THE RECORD

Jim Laker was born at Bradford on 9 February 1922. He took 1,944 wickets (average 21.24) in his first-class career (1946–64). Along with his 'spin twin' and pal, Tony Lock, he played a key role in Surrey's seven successive championship victories from 1952. He took 193 wickets in 46 Tests, including a record 46 in the 1956 series against Australia. Jim wound down his distinguished career with Essex and is now a *Daily Express* cricket writer and the Voice of Cricket on BBC in partnership with another legendary spinner, Richie Benaud.

BARRY NORMAN'S
DREAM TEAM

  1 LEN HUTTON
  2 DAVID GOWER
  3 PETER MAY
  4 DENIS COMPTON
  5 KEN BARRINGTON
  6 IAN BOTHAM
  7 GODFREY EVANS
  8 JOHNNY WARDLE
  9 JIM LAKER
 10 FRED TRUEMAN
 11 FRANK TYSON

'I've deliberately restricted myself to English players because, dammit, I *always* cheer for England. Even so, it was not an easy choice. No room, you see, for Dexter, Statham, Tony Lock, Alan Knott or even – shameful – the great Tom Graveney, although I considered them all very deeply. Gower might seem an odd choice for opener (no Boycott? no Washbrook?) but the right- and left-hander combination appeals to me and, besides, David virtually opens for England now, so he might as well do the job from the start. Tyson instead of Statham? That was difficult, especially as in the long term Statham was almost certainly the better bowler. But my assumption was that by some miracle all these players would be brought together when each was at his very best and, for a brief time, Tyson was I think the best and fastest of our post-war bowlers. I reckon my selection would beat any team from any other period or any other country, especially if Botham was in his untouchable 1981 form . . .'

BARRY NORMAN

BARRY NORMAN has been anchoring the BBC-TV film series since 1972 apart from a short break during which he went into bat for Omnibus. A first-rate writer with a distinguished Fleet Street career behind him, Barry describes himself as 'a cricket nut'.

DEREK RANDALL'S
TEN GREATEST FIELDERS

1 **DAVID GOWER** *(England, 1975–   )*
2 **KEN TAYLOR** *(England, 1953–68)*
3 **CLIVE LLOYD** *(West Indies, 1963–   )*

4 **PHIL SHARPE** *(England, 1958–76)*
5 **BASHARAT HASSAN** *(Kenya, 1964–)*
6 **COLIN BLAND** *(South Africa, 1956–73)*
7 **TONY GREIG** *(England, 1965–80)*
8 **VIV RICHARDS** *(West Indies, 1971–)*
9 **IAN BOTHAM** *(England, 1974–)*
10 **BOBBY SIMPSON** *(Australia, 1952–78)*

'My selections are not given in any particular order. I have picked Gower for his elegance and brilliance; Taylor for his effortless ease and mobility; Lloyd for being spectacular and powerfully deceptive; Phil Sharpe for his razor sharp reflexes; Basharat Hassan, fearless and with lightning reactions that make him ideal for the bat-pad catches; Bland for his pin-point throwing accuracy; Greig because he's got hands like buckets and I never saw him drop a catch; Richards and Botham for their all-round magnificence in the field; Simpson because his 110 catches in 62 Tests reveal what safe hands he had.'

DEREK RANDALL

TOM GRAVENEY: 'There has rarely been a cover-point to match Derek for speed of thought and action. He is worth a place in any team for the runs he saves in the field, let alone his prolific scoring. His acrobatics when fielding can be entertaining for the spectators, inspiring for his team-mates and disconcerting for the batsmen who find potential boundaries suddenly turned into suicidal singles.'

FOR THE RECORD

Derek Randall was born at Retford, Notts, on 24 February 1951. He made his debut for Notts in 1972 and has had an up-and-down career with England, punctuated with moments of brilliance and occasional mediocrity with the bat, but he has never been anything less than stunning in the field. He will always be remembered for one of the greatest Test innings of modern times when he drove, hooked and cut his way to 174 priceless runs in the Centenary Test against Australia in Melbourne in 1977. Derek is one of the game's great characters and is a crowd favourite at every ground because of his enthusiasm and his ability to light up the dullest game.

BASIL D'OLIVEIRA'S
TEN GREATEST BATTLERS

1 **BARRY RICHARDS** *(South Africa, 1964–)*
2 **GEOFF BOYCOTT** *(England, 1962–)*
3 **GRAHAM GOOCH** *(England, 1973–)*
4 **ROHAN KANHAI** *(West Indies, 1955–77)*
5 **VIV RICHARDS** *(West Indies, 1971–)*
6 **GRAEME POLLOCK** *(South Africa, 1960–)*
7 **ZAHEER ABBAS** *(Pakistan, 1965–)*
8 **GREG CHAPPELL** *(Australia, 1966–)*
9 **COLIN COWDREY** *(England, 1950–76)*
10 **GARFIELD SOBERS** *(West Indies, 1953–74)*

'As well as marvellous ability, all these batsmen were also blessed with great fighting qualities. They could break the hearts of bowlers with their competitive spirit, battling on regardless of what was thrown at them and scoring runs in even the most tense situations and on the worst sort of playing surfaces when the ball was flying off at all angles and heights. They are the sort of batsmen a captain prays for in moments of crisis and all had remarkable powers of concentration.'

BASIL D'OLIVEIRA

TOM GRAVENEY: 'Basil was a great all-rounder who graced the cricket field with his genius for the game but I shall always remember him for his battling spirit in backs-to-the-wall situations. He was Mr Unflappable who would never concede defeat until the final ball had been bowled. Basil was a real fighter who used to lift the players around him with his determined approach to every game.'

FOR THE RECORD

Basil D'Oliveira was born in Cape Town on 12 February 1942. He was the first coloured South African cricketer to overcome the primitive conditions in which he was compelled to play at home and to emerge as a world star. Thanks largely to the efforts of John Arlott and Peter Walker, he came to England in 1960 to join Middleton in the Lancashire League before becoming a magnificent player for Worcestershire from 1965 until his retirement in 1979. An immensely talented all-rounder, he scored 18,882 runs at an average 39.66 and took 548 wickets at an average 27.38. He amassed 2,484 runs and took 47 wickets in 44 Tests for England and always conducted himself with great dignity despite being in the centre of controversy because of South Africa's apartheid system.

TED DEXTER'S
TEN GREATEST STROKE PLAYERS

1 **GARFIELD SOBERS** *(West Indies, 1953–74)*
2 **GRAEME POLLOCK** *(South Africa, 1960–   )*
3 **VIV RICHARDS** *(West Indies, 1971–   )*
4 **BARRY RICHARDS** *(South Africa, 1964–   )*
5 **PETER BURGE** *(Australia, 1952–68)*
6 **COLIN MILBURN** *(England, 1960–74)*
7 **NAWAB OF PATAUDI** *(India, 1957–76)*
8 **GEORGE EMMETT** *(England, 1936–59)*
9 **JIM PARKS** *(England, 1949–75)*
10 **PETER MAY** *(England, 1948–63)*

'I have concentrated my choice on players from my own era. All were a delight to watch for the fluency and range of their strokes. They are not listed in any particular order except Sobers at number one. He was a true master with the bat, a natural stroke player who demonstrated a fine balance between power and relaxation.'

TED DEXTER

TOM GRAVENEY: 'Ted Dexter – "Lord" Ted – was a gifted cricketer with an adventurous spirit. He didn't believe in hanging around at the wicket. Every ball was there to be hit and he could be quite majestic when taking an attack apart with a bombardment of stunning shots. He is also a classical strokemaker on the golf course! I agree, of course, with his choice of Garfield Sobers as No. 1 in this list. He not only had all the ability in the world but was also exciting and explosive to watch, no matter what the state of the game.'

FOR THE RECORD

Ted Dexter was born in Milan on 15 May 1935. He captained Cambridge University, Sussex and England during a career (1956–68) in which he scored 4,502 runs in 62 Tests and took 66 wickets. His highest Test and career score was 205 for England against Pakistan in Karachi in 1961–62. A Cambridge Blue at cricket and golf, he was rated one of Britain's finest amateur golfers. His best bowling analysis was seven for 24 for Sussex against Middlesex. He is a regular BBC-TV summariser and writes a weekly column during the cricket season for the *Sunday Mirror*.

LANCE GIBBS'S
TEN GREATEST SPIN BOWLERS

1 **RICHIE BENAUD** *(Australia, 1948–64)*
2 **'FERGIE' GUPTE** *(India, 1947–63)*
3 **SONNY RAMADHIN** *(West Indies, 1949–65)*
4 **ALF VALENTINE** *(West Indies, 1949–64)*
5 **JIM LAKER** *(England, 1946–64)*
6 **BISHEN BEDI** *(India, 1961–   )*
7 **HUGH TAYFIELD** *(South Africa, 1945–62)*
8 **BHAGWAT CHANDRASEKHAR** *(India, 1963–   )*
9 **DEREK UNDERWOOD** *(England, 1963–   )*
10 **ERAPALLY PRASANNA** *(India, 1961–   )*

'I found this very difficult and have stuck to players that I had the pleasure of seeing in action. They were all masters of spin and able to make the ball turn sharply on any surface. Another thing they had in common was deadly accuracy and they all had the ability to vary the flight and pace of their deliveries.'

LANCE GIBBS

TOM GRAVENEY: 'Lance had what was then a world record 309 Test wickets as testimony to his talent as an off-spinner who could produce startling spin and bounce. He would bound in to bowl off a five-pace run-up and used his long fingers to give the ball an extra tweak as it left his hand. A man of incredible stamina, Lance could bowl all day and his variations of pace meant that no batsman dare relax against him.'

FOR THE RECORD

Lancelot Gibbs was born at Georgetown, British Guyana, on 29 September 1934. A counsin of Clive Lloyd, he took 1,024 wickets at an average 27.22 in a career (1953–76) during which he played for Guyana and Warwickshire. His 309 wickets in 79

Tests was a world record until Dennis Lillee overtook him. He was a genuine tail-end batsman but was worth a place in any team for his fielding alone. A specialist in the gully position, he held 203 catches including 52 in Test matches. His best bowling return was eight for 38 in a Test against India in Barbados in 1961–62. All eight wickets fell during a 15.3 over spell in which he conceded just six runs and bowled 14 maidens.

COLIN MILBURN'S
TEN GREATEST ENTERTAINERS

1 **GARFIELD SOBERS** *(West Indies, 1953–74)*
2 **VIV RICHARDS** *(West Indies, 1971–   )*
3 **BARRY RICHARDS** *(South Africa, 1964–   )*
4 **GRAEME POLLOCK** *(South Africa, 1960–   )*
5 **TED DEXTER** *(England, 1956–68)*
6 **NORMAN O'NEILL** *(Australia, 1955–67)*
7 **GREG CHAPPELL** *(Australia, 1966–   )*
8 **DAVID GOWER** *(England, 1975–   )*
9 **IAN BOTHAM** *(England, 1974–   )*
10 **ROHAN KANHAI** *(West Indies, 1955–77)*

'These are listed in the order they came to my memory and I have selected only from batsmen that I have either played with or at least seen. It's my opinion that you couldn't find ten more entertaining batsmen from any era. Naturally Garry Sobers came quickly to my mind. Any player who can set and reach a target of six sixes off six consecutive balls has to be a king entertainer.'

COLIN MILBURN

TOM GRAVENEY: '"Ollie" Milburn was a big cricket hero in every sense. Big in bulk, big in heart, big in talent and big in popularity. He weighed more than 18 stone and he poured every ounce of his considerable strength into his shots. His savage hooking and cutting won him an army of fans and it was a tragedy for Colin in particular and cricket in general when he lost an eye in a car accident in 1969. He was a marvellous entertainer.'

FOR THE RECORD

Colin Milburn was born in Burnopfield, Co. Durham, on 23 October 1941. He started his first-class career with Northants in 1960 and made a brief comeback in 1973 following the tragic car smash that put him out of the game at the peak of his powers. His vintage year was 1966 when he amassed 1,861 runs at an average 48.97. His run barrage that summer included a century before lunch in three matches and a hurricane innings of 203 against Essex at Clacton. He scored 13,262 runs at an average 33.07, including 23 centuries. His average in nine Tests was 46.71. He was a useful medium-pace bowler and claimed 99 first-class wickets.

JOHN ARLOTT'S
DREAM TEAM

  1 JACK HOBBS
  2 MIKE BREARLEY
  3 GEORGE BROWN
  4 TOM GRAVENEY
  5 GARFIELD SOBERS
  6 KEITH MILLER
  7 LEO HARRISON
  8 JIM LAKER
  9 FRANK TYSON
10 BILL BOWES
11 ARTHUR MAILEY

'I would describe this as my team of favourites. They are listed in batting order and I contend that they would probably be good enough to beat any other eleven. Leo Harrison, 'The Lion' of Hampshire, is the only member of the team who did not play Test cricket, more's the pity. He was a true cricketer's cricketer with a marvellous dry humour. He would catch an opposing batsman behind the wicket and then say to his victim: 'Hard luck, mate: ain't half a bloody game, eh . . .' He was good enough in his youth to be described as "the new Bradman" but the cricketer he might have been became a war casualty. By the mid-1950s and after only two seasons as a regular wicket-keeper he was clearly among the best in the country, probably second only to Godfrey Evans. His handling was sweetly clean and he had a deep love for the game that shone through in everything that he did.'

JOHN ARLOTT

JOHN ARLOTT, the Voice of Cricket, would top all lists as the No. 1 commentator on the game. He was The Master of the microphone and his retirement from the BBC radio's Test commentary team for the peace of his beloved Alderney left a hole that can never be filled. Tom Graveney comments: 'John Arlott was the Cricket Voice for All Seasons. We will never hear his like again. His descriptive word pictures brought the game of cricket to life for millions of listeners.'

BRIAN STATHAM'S
TEN GREATEST NEW BALL PARTNERS

1 **HAROLD LARWOOD and BILL VOCE** *(England)*
2 **RAY LINDWALL and KEITH MILLER** *(Australia)*
3 **DENNIS LILLEE and JEFF THOMSON** *(Australia)*
4 **WES HALL and CHARLIE GRIFFITH** *(West Indies)*
5 **MICHAEL HOLDING and ANDY ROBERTS** *(West Indies)*
6 **ALEC BEDSER and PETER LOADER** *(England)*
7 **PETER HEINE and NEIL ADCOCK** *(South Africa)*
8 **ALAN DAVIDSON and GRAHAM McKENZIE** *(Australia)*
9 **PETER POLLOCK and MIKE PROCTER** *(South Africa)*
10 **LES JACKSON and CLIFF GLADWIN** *(England)*

'I did not have the good fortune to see Larwood and Voce in action but from the stories I have been told by their contemporaries they must have been sheer dynamite together. I have selected two great County combinations – Bedser and Loader, who did so much to make Surrey supreme in the 1950s, and Jackson and Gladwin, who wrecked the best batting sides when they got them on those green wickets of Derbyshire. A pair I would loved to have seen in harness at their peak are my old partners Fred Trueman and Frank Tyson. That would have been quite a spectacle, except for the batsmen on the receiving end!'

BRIAN STATHAM

TOM GRAVENEY: 'Brian was a classical fast bowler whose nagging accuracy set batsmen up for the "kill" by partners like Fred Trueman and Frank Tyson. They were more hostile but could not match Brian's deadly line and length. He was a captain's dream, always prepared to bowl himself into the ground for the team.'

FOR THE RECORD

Brian Statham – George to his friends – was born in Manchester on 16 June 1930. In an 18-year career (1950–68) he took 2,260 wickets at an average 16.36, including 252 wickets in 70 Tests. He took more than 100 wickets in a season 13 times and performed the hat-trick three times. He captained Lancashire for two years at the tail-end of his career and twice took 15 wickets in County matches – against Warwickshire in 1957 and against Leicestershire in 1964.

FAROKH ENGINEER'S
TEN GREATEST WICKET-KEEPERS

1 **KEITH ANDREW** *(England, 1952–66)*
2 **ALAN KNOTT** *(England, 1964–   )*
3 **BOB TAYLOR** *(England, 1960–   )*
4 **JACKIE HENDRIKS** *(West Indies, 1953–72)*
5 **GODFREY EVANS** *(England, 1939–59)*
6 **WALLY GROUT** *(Australia, 1946–66)*
7 **DON TALLON** *(Australia, 1933–54)*
8 **GIL LANGLEY** *(Australia, 1945–57)*
9 **WASIM BARI** *(Pakistan, 1965–   )*
10 **RODNEY MARSH** *(Australia, 1968–   )*

'I juggled with short-lists that included players such as Syed Kirmani, John Waite and Alan (A.C.) Smith before arriving at this line-up. Keith Andrew tops my list because he was a real player's player who made the art of wicket-keeping look easy. He had a beautiful pair of hands and was totally reliable whether standing up to the stumps or back to the pacemen.'

FAROKH ENGINEER

TOM GRAVENEY: 'Farokh "Rooky" Engineer is one of the greatest wicket-keepers India has produced. He was acrobatic and had tremendously fast reflexes, getting to the ball and removing the bails in a flash if the batsman's foot was raised. Farokh was also a top-flight batsman and served both India and Lancashire with distinction.'

FOR THE RECORD

Farokh Engineer was born in Bombay on 25 February 1938. He made his debut for Bombay in 1959–60 and eight years later started a successful association with Lancashire. He scored 13,436 runs in first-class cricket and caught 703 batsmen and made 121 stumpings. In 46 Tests he totalled 2,611 runs and made 82 dismissals. He was a powerful batsman who was at home either opening the innings or playing an aggressive role in the middle order. His highest Test score was 121 against England at Bombay in 1972–73.

BOBBY SIMPSON'S
TEN GREATEST SLIP CATCHERS

1. **NEIL HARVEY** (*Australia, 1942–62*)
2. **GREG CHAPPELL** (*Australia, 1966– *)
3. **IAN CHAPPELL** (*Australia, 1961–80*)
4. **PHIL SHARPE** (*England, 1958–76*)
5. **COLIN COWDREY** (*England, 1950–76*)
6. **KEN BARRINGTON** (*England, 1953–68*)
7. **GARFIELD SOBERS** (*West Indies, 1953–74*)
8. **KEITH MILLER** (*Australia, 1937–59*)
9. **MIKE BREARLEY** (*England, 1961–81*)
10. **IAN BOTHAM** (*England, 1974– *)

'All these players were capable of bringing off the "impossible" catches that can swing matches. They had lightning reflexes and the sight of them crouched close to the wicket would inspire the bowlers to produce that vital extra effort. Neil Harvey was at his best in the covers but could also produce brilliant work in the slips.'

BOBBY SIMPSON

TOM GRAVENEY: 'Next to Wally Hammond, Bobby Simpson is the greatest slip fielder I've seen. He had safe hands and incredibly quick reactions. In 62 Tests, he held 110 catches and he could bring off the sort of blinding catches that could lift the morale of his team-mates and suddenly change the course of a game.'

FOR THE RECORD

Bobby Simpson was born in Sydney of Scottish parents on 3 February 1936. A magnificent all-rounder for New South Wales and then Western Australia, he captained Australia in 29 Tests between 1963–64 and 1967–68 and then in another ten Tests when making a comeback to the international arena following the mass defections to World Series Cricket. He scored 21,029 runs during his career (1952–78), including 4,869 runs in 62 Tests. His highest Test score was 311 against England at Old Trafford in 1964. He got a triple ton in the same year for New South Wales, scoring 359 against Queensland. The following year he amassed 201 runs when sharing a record opening stand of 382 with Bill Lawry against West Indies in Bridgetown.

JOHN LEVER'S
TEN GREATEST LEFT-ARM FAST BOWLERS

1 **GARFIELD SOBERS** *(West Indies, 1953–74)*
2 **ALAN DAVIDSON** *(Australia, 1949–63)*
3 **TREVOR GODDARD** *(South Africa, 1952–69)*
4 **BILL JOHNSTON** *(Australia, 1945–54)*
5 **JEFF JONES** *(England, 1960–68)*
6 **FRED RUMSEY** *(England, 1960–70)*
7 **GARY GILMOUR** *(Australia, 1971–   )*
8 **RICHARD COLLINGE** *(New Zealand, 1963–   )*
9 **BERNARD JULIEN** *(West Indies, 1966–77)*
10 **TONY LOCK** *(when bowling his quicker ball!!)*

'Garry Sobers was not the quickest of bowlers but could give the greatest batsmen problems with his prodigious swing. Alan Davidson started off specialising in bowling "chinamen" but then developed into one of Australia's quickest and deadliest pacemen. I did not see Bill Johnston in action but I am told he could get lift and real pace on the tamest of wickets.'

                                                    JOHN LEVER

TOM GRAVENEY: 'It took John Lever a long time to get the recognition he deserved as more than just a good-class County bowler. I feel he has been unlucky not to have played many more times for England. He has a nagging accuracy and can move the ball off the pitch and in the air. His swing can deceive the finest batsmen.'

FOR THE RECORD

John Lever was born in Stepney on 24 February 1949. He started his first-class career with Essex in 1967 but it was ten years before he won an England cap, making a stunning debut against India. On his first day in Test cricket he scored 53 runs and took four wickets for 16 runs, finishing the match with ten for 70. He took

106 wickets for an average 15.80 in 1978 and produced almost identical figures in 1979 to inspire Essex's first County championship triumph. His best figures were eight for 49 against Warwickshire in 1979. An outstanding fielder, he has taken 60 wickets in 18 Tests.

DEREK UNDERWOOD'S
TEN GREATEST LEFT-ARM SPIN BOWLERS

1 **BISHEN BEDI** *(India, 1961–82)*
2 **TONY LOCK** *(England, 1946–71)*
3 **NORMAN GIFFORD** *(England, 1960–   )*
4 **ALF VALENTINE** *(West Indies, 1949–64)*
5 **PHIL EDMONDS** *(England, 1971–   )*
6 **JOHNNY WARDLE** *(England, 1946–58)*
7 **DON WILSON** *(England, 1957–74)*
8 **GARFIELD SOBERS** *(West Indies, 1953–74)*
9 **GEORGE TRIBE** *(Australia, 1945–59)*
10 **'VINOO' MANKAD** *(India, 1935–63)*

'Sam Cook, Peter Sainsbury, Tufty Mann and Hedley Howarth were among others who came to mind as I struggled to finalise my list. Of the old school, I understand Hedley Verity was a supreme left-arm spinner but I have stuck to bowlers who have been in action in post-war years. Garfield Sobers gets in because, although better known for his swing bowling, he did start out as a deadly accurate spinner.'

DEREK UNDERWOOD

TOM GRAVENEY: 'Fittingly nicknamed "Deadly" because of his uncanny accuracy, Derek Underwood is an invaluable team stalwart who can stifle the most adventurous batsmen on good wickets and trick and trap the finest technicians on any surface that offers him the slightest help and encouragement. His pace is normally slow-medium but he adjusts it to suit the conditions and at times sends down deliveries that are very nearly medium fast. He would be No. 1 in my top ten list of left-arm spinners.'

FOR THE RECORD

Derek Underwood was born at Bromley, Kent, on 8 June 1945. He has taken more than 2,000 wickets since starting his first-class career with Kent in 1963. He was just 17 and in his first season became the youngest bowler ever to take 100 wickets. His best bowling return was nine for 28 for Kent against Sussex at Hastings in 1964. He has taken 297 wickets in 86 Test matches.

ERIC SYKES'S
DREAM TEAM

1 SIR DON BRADMAN
2 VIV RICHARDS
3 IAN BOTHAM
4 DENIS COMPTON
5 CLIVE LLOYD
6 MIKE BREARLEY
7 GODFREY EVANS
8 FREDDIE, sorry . . . JIM LAKER
9 FRED TRUEMAN
10 WES HALL
11 JIM THIGHS

'I can hear them asking in the Long Room and the smallest room in the house . . . Jim Thighs? Who's he? Jim is a pal of mine. He has only got one leg which makes it difficult to get him LBW. I reckon that if Mike Brearley can make this side, then there's hope for Jim. After Bradman and Viv Richards have opened all hours and then Botham, Compton and Lloyd have got stuck into the bowling the only question will be one of the timing of the declaration. Then fiery Fred Trueman and Wes "The Whirlwind" Hall will share the new ball, with Botham and Jim Laker taking over to clear up the tail-enders. With Godders diving around behind the stumps, there will be few extras conceded. It is truly a dream team that will make the opposition think they are having a nightmare.'

ERIC SYKES

ERIC SYKES, talented scriptwriter, comedian and comedy actor, is a keen charity cricketer who specialises in keeping wicket. He was once described as being just like Evans behind the stumps. Godfrey? No, Dame Edith. Eric takes his cricket seriously and has a permanent bump on his finger to prove it. He broke a finger when taking a snorter behind the wicket from Fred Rumsey.

BISHOP DAVID SHEPPARD'S
TEN GREATEST BATSMEN

1 **DR W. G. GRACE** *(England, 1865–1908)*
2 **JACK HOBBS** *(England, 1905–34)*
3 **VICTOR TRUMPER** *(Australia, 1884–1914)*
4 **DON BRADMAN** *(Australia, 1927–49)*
5 **LEN HUTTON** *(England, 1934–60)*

6 **EVERTON WEEKES** *(West Indies, 1944–64)*
7 **PETER MAY** *(England, 1948–63)*
8 **GARFIELD SOBERS** *(West Indies, 1953–74)*
9 **VIV RICHARDS** *(West Indies, 1971–   )*
10 **GREG CHAPPELL** *(Australia, 1966–   )*

'Perhaps the most difficult task was deciding which of the "Three W's" to choose – Walcott, Worrell or Weekes, all of whom were masters of the batting art. In the end I plumped for Everton Weekes, who in his greatest days would throw the bat at the ball with sheer exuberance and a succession of strokes would stream out that no one else would attempt. He was built small, very like Bradman, and I guess he played more like Bradman at his best than any other player I saw.'

DAVID SHEPPARD

TOM GRAVENEY: 'David was a graceful off-side player and an opener of the highest calibre who had enormous powers of concentration. He was a thoughtful captain of Cambridge University and Sussex and led England in two Tests against Pakistan. Now, of course, best known as the Bishop of Liverpool, David always represented cricket with great dignity and style and it was a privilege to play with him.'

FOR THE RECORD

The Rt Rev. David Sheppard, Bishop of Liverpool, was born in Reigate, Surrey, on 6 March 1929. He scored 15,838 runs at an average 43.51, including 45 centuries, and captained Cambridge University, Sussex and England during an eventful career (1947–63). In 1952 he scored 127 in the University match and topped the national first-class batting average with 2,262 runs at an average 64.62. During that memorable season he scored a career-best 239 not out for Cambridge against Worcester. He was the first ordained minister to play in Test cricket.

COLIN COWDREY'S
TEN GREATEST TEST GROUNDS

1. **LORD'S,** *London*
2. **NEWLANDS,** *Capetown*
3. **ADELAIDE OVAL,** *South Australia*
4. **MELBOURNE,** *Victoria*
5. **SYDNEY,** *New South Wales*
6. **CHRISTCHURCH,** *New Zealand*
7. **PORT-OF-SPAIN,** *Trinidad*
8. **LAHORE,** *Pakistan*
9. **EDEN GARDENS,** *Calcutta*
10. **SABINA PARK,** *Jamaica*

'It's cruel tying me down to just ten when I enjoyed my cricket at so many wonderful grounds around the world. I could have mentioned Old Trafford, Kingsmead in Durban, Bombay, Bangalore and Salisbury and so many more. One of the most spectacular grounds I played at – although not in Test cricket – was in the beautiful setting of Colombo. I have not made my selection in any particular order but if I had to be pinned down to naming my favourite ground away from the Test area I would select Canterbury. It is countrified and has a festival atmosphere that makes it a pleasure for players and spectators alike.'

COLIN COWDREY

TOM GRAVENEY: 'Colin was a masterly batsman, with excellent technique and a vast array of elegant strokes. He was also a much under-rated skipper. I would rate him the best captain under whom I ever toured, particularly in the West Indies in 1968. You have to respect his ratings of the world's Test grounds because he played in just about every one of them during his distinguished career. Lord's would top my list because it is the home of cricket and has a unique atmosphere. You can *feel* the tradition and history just by walking into the ground.'

FOR THE RECORD

Michael Colin Cowdrey, deliberately given the initials MCC by his cricket-loving father, was born in Bangalore, India, on 24 December 1932. He played in a world record 114 Tests and amassed 7,624 runs at an average 44.06 in one of the greatest of all cricket careers (1950–75). He scored more than 1,000 runs 27 times on his way to a career total of 42,719 and carved out two centuries in a match on three occasions. Captain of Oxford University, he later skippered Kent from 1957 until 1971 and led them to the County championship in 1970. He was a magnificent slip fielder, holding 638 catches including 120 in Tests.

BOB TAYLOR'S
TEN GREATEST WICKET-KEEPERS

1 **KEITH ANDREW** *(England, 1952–66)*
2 **GODFREY EVANS** *(England, 1939–59)*
3 **WALLY GROUT** *(Australia, 1946–66)*
4 **DON TALLON** *(Australia, 1933–54)*
5 **ALAN KNOTT** *(England, 1964–   )*
6 **RODNEY MARSH** *(Australia, 1968–   )*
7 **BERTIE OLDFIELD** *(Australia, 1919–38)*
8 **SYED KIRMANI** *(India, 1967–   )*
9 **WASIM BARI** *(Pakistan, 1965–   )*
10 **ARTHUR McINTYRE** *(England, 1938–63)*

'I have put Don Tallon and Bertie Oldfield in my list on the strength of stories I have been told about their great ability by cricketers who played with and against them. Keith Andrew gets number one place because he was a model wicket-keeper with the sort of skills we all try to emulate. He was a purist of a player – unspectacular but totally reliable.'

BOB TAYLOR

TOM GRAVENEY: 'There have been few, if any, more accomplished wicket-keepers than Bob Taylor. He would I think be the choice of most pros in the game as the best in the business. He was unlucky to have to live in Alan Knott's shadow for many years but has now firmly established himself as one of the finest 'keepers to have crouched behind the stumps for England. Few can match him for agility, consistency and dedication.'

FOR THE RECORD

Bob Taylor was born in Stoke on 17 July 1941. He started his first-class career with Derbyshire in 1960 and has dismissed more than 1,500 batsmen with wicket-keeping that earns him the admiration even of his victims. A former professional footballer with Port Vale, he caught ten Hampshire batsmen in a match at Chesterfield in 1963. His seven dismissals in an innings and ten in the match against India in the 1980 Golden Jubilee Test in Bombay were a world record. He is a useful right-hand bat who has featured in several stubborn stands for England.

RAY LINDWALL'S
TEN GREATEST FAST BOWLERS

1 **HAROLD LARWOOD** (*England, 1924–38*)
2 **DENNIS LILLEE** (*Australia, 1945–60*)
3 **FRED TRUEMAN** (*England, 1949–69*)
4 **KEITH MILLER** (*Australia, 1937–59*)
5 **WES HALL** (*West Indies, 1955–71*)

6 MICHAEL HOLDING *(West Indies, 1972–   )*
7 FRANK TYSON *(England, 1952–60)*
8 ALAN DAVIDSON *(Australia, 1949–63)*
9 BILL JOHNSTON *(Australia, 1945–54)*
10 JEFF THOMSON *(Australia, 1972–   )*

'It was harder deciding which bowlers to leave out than which to put in. The likes of Richard Hadlee, Brian Statham, Imran Khan and Andy Roberts were all given careful consideration and could easily have made it into my top ten. I have put Harold Larwood in first place because of the enormous impact he had on the game when I was just a schoolboy. I watched him bowl in the "bodyline" series and never forgot the experience. He had a model action and was almost unplayable at his peak.'

RAY LINDWALL

TOM GRAVENEY: 'For me, Ray Lindwall has been the world's No. 1 fast bowler of the post-war era. He had genuine pace and even when at top speed had full control of the ball. At his best when partnered by Keith Miller, Lindwall was always beautifully balanced at delivery, could swing the ball both ways and was a marvellously competitive player. He was a determined but sporting opponent who went about his job without fuss or histrionics.'

FOR THE RECORD

Ray Lindwall was born at Mascot, Sydney, on 3 October 1921. As well as being one of the greatest fast bowlers of all time he was also an attacking batsman who scored 5,017 runs during his career (1945–60). In 61 Tests, he took 228 wickets at an average 23.03. He played for New South Wales and Queensland and had a total wickets haul of 794 at an average 21.33. He was particularly devastating against England, capturing 114 wickets in 29 Tests.

SECTION TWO
HEROES OF THE HEROES

Fifty Test players name the players that they have idolised

DENNIS AMISS
Warwickshire (1960–)

MY CHILDHOOD BATTING HERO
For me, Denis Compton was the big shining light of cricket. He excited thousands of schoolboys with his batting feats and I was no exception. There was a magic in his play and an approach to the game that had an almost magnetic attraction.

MY CHILDHOOD BOWLING HERO
Alec Bedser was the mainstay of the England attack when I first started to take a close interest in cricket and I always looked for his performances. There have been few better or bigger-hearted medium-fast bowlers before or since.

MY IDEA OF THE PERFECT BATSMAN
I have never lost my schoolboy admiration for Denis Compton. He was a genius who had everything. Once he had got his eye in he would murder the bowling with a variety of shots, some classical and others that were wonderfully inventive and not found in any coaching manual.

MY IDEA OF THE PERFECT BOWLER
For pace and accuracy I pick Dennis Lillee and John Snow. Both maintained a magnificent line, attacking the off stump and making the ball leave the pitch at tremendous speed. Both had an aggressive attitude which

meant they were always menacing the batsmen and they each had a classic action. For slow bowlers, Jim Laker and Bishen Bedi were the kings. They had tremendous control of flight and superb wrist and finger action.

FOR THE RECORD

Dennis Amiss was born at Harborne, Birmingham, on 7 April 1943. He averaged 46.30 in 50 Tests for England. He made his County debut for Warwickshire at the age of 17 and had his most prolific season with the bat in 1976 when he amassed 2,110 runs at an average 65.93. A defiant and stylish opener, he scored 11 Tests centuries including a double ton against the West Indies in 1976.

TREVOR BAILEY
Essex (1945–67)

MY CHILDHOOD BATTING HERO
Don Bradman, who was such a power in the game when I was first starting my love affair with cricket. You only have to count the runs he scored and the regularity with which he scored them to understand why he was a hero to so many people, young and old alike.

MY CHILDHOOD BOWLING HERO
Harold Larwood, who appealed to me simply because at the time he was the fastest and most exciting bowler in the world. His performances in the 'bodyline' series in Australia helped hook this nine-year-old to cricket!

MY IDEA OF THE PERFECT BATSMAN
Don Bradman. He won so many Tests by the runs he scored and the pace at which he collected them. As well as

his mastery of batting, he also had one of the most astute tactical brains the game has ever seen, expert at discerning weaknesses in the opposition and exploiting them to the full.

MY IDEA OF THE PERFECT BOWLER

Sydney Barnes, whose figures speak for themselves as to his great ability. In 132 first-class matches he took five or more wickets in an innings on no fewer than 68 occasions!

FOR THE RECORD

Trevor Bailey was born at Westcliff, Essex, on 3 December 1923. He was a brilliant all-rounder, scoring 2,290 runs in 61 Tests and taking 132 wickets with lively medium-pace bowling. Captain of Essex from 1961 until 1967, his many stubborn performances as a fiercely competitive batsman – particularly against Australia – earned him the nickname 'Barnacle'. But he could also get runs in a hurry as he proved in a partnership with Essex colleague Doug Insole when they both scored a century before lunch against Notts. He was a double Blue at Cambridge, winning an FA Amateur Cup medal with Walthamstow Avenue in 1952. Trevor is now a perceptive cricket correspondent with the *Financial Times* and an expert summariser on BBC Radio's not-to-be-missed *Test Match Special* programme.

ALEC BEDSER
Surrey (1939–60)

MY CHILDHOOD BOWLING HERO

I had three particular favourites, Harold Larwood, Maurice Tate and the great Australian leg spinner Bill 'Tiger' O'Reilly. They were the 'tops' when I was a youngster and each of them excited me with bowling that was always deadly accurate and often devastating.

MY CHILDHOOD BATTING HERO
Sir Jack Hobbs and Walter Hammond did most to capture my imagination. Both were masters of the game with excellent technique and a full range of strokes that meant they could amass runs on any surface.

MY IDEA OF THE PERFECT BOWLER
Larwood, Tate and O'Reilly spring to mind again. The perfect bowler is one who has control of length and direction and change of pace and, if a slow bowler, variation of flight. Larwood, Tate and O'Reilly were all remarkably accurate as well as being deadly on any pitch that offered the slightest assistance.

MY IDEA OF THE PERFECT BATSMAN
I can't be pinned down on this one. Hobbs and Hammond came as close to perfection as you can possibly get and there has been a whole array of batsmen since the war with a vast repertoire of strokes.

FOR THE RECORD

See page 28

IAN BOTHAM
Somerset (1975–   )

MY CHILDHOOD BATTING HERO
The one and only Garry Sobers. He was the cricketer who captured my imagination when I was a youngster, with both the bat and the ball. I liked his approach to the game and my earliest ambition was to become an all-rounder in

his mould. Cricket was always enjoyable when Garry was out in the middle, whether he was batting or bowling.

MY CHILDHOOD BOWLING HERO
Wes Hall was the bowler whose performances used to excite me. He was spectacularly fast and was a danger to batsmen even on docile wickets. When he and Charlie Griffith were sharing the new ball, West Indies were always in with a chance of picking up quick wickets.

MY IDEA OF THE PERFECT BATSMAN
It's got to be Viv Richards. When he's really motoring he can dominate any attack in the world. He always goes for his shots and gives spectators great value for their money. Whether hammering the ball or stroking it, he is a master at placing it to beat the tightest field.

MY IDEA OF THE PERFECT BOWLER
Dennis Lillee, who has been such a magnificent servant for Australia. He can be as quick as anybody in the world but is equally dangerous when bowling at a slower pace because of his ability to move the ball either way off the pitch or in the air. And what a competitor!

FOR THE RECORD

Ian Botham was born at Heswall, Cheshire, on 24 November 1955. He won his County cap with Somerset in 1976 and was the following season elected Best Young Cricketer of the Year by the Cricket Writers' Club. Playing against Pakistan at Lord's in 1978, he became the first player ever to take eight Test wickets in an innings and score 100 in the same match. His highest score is 228, for Somerset against Gloucestershire in 1980. He is one of the most exciting and gifted cricketers in the world and his performances with the bat and the ball against Australia in the 1981 Test series lifted him into the land of cricketing legend. Almost single-handed, he turned a series that seemed lost in England's favour with some devastating batting and bowling. In the 1980 Jubilee Test against India in Bombay, Botham scored

114 runs and took 13 wickets. He is a man for all seasons and on all wickets. Botham is also a good-class footballer who is on Scunthorpe United's books.

BRIAN CLOSE
Yorkshire and Somerset (1949–78)

MY CHILDHOOD BATTING HERO
Len Hutton. When I was a youngster growing up in Yorkshire, Len Hutton was a god in our community. I was fortunate enough to later play with him for Yorkshire and never had reason to change my assessment of him. It was a pleasure and privilege to be in the same team.

MY CHILDHOOD BOWLING HERO
Bill Bowes was the bowler I idolised. He was the spearhead of the Yorkshire attack and could make the ball kick and bounce on even the most docile wickets. His bowling was often hostile but also intelligent.

MY IDEA OF THE PERFECT BATSMAN
It has to be Len Hutton. He was and had everything. For me, he was attractive to watch scoring a few runs in a long time as anyone else scoring a lot in a short spell.

MY IDEA OF THE PERFECT BOWLER
J. H. (Johnny) Wardle was as close as you can get to being perfect. He was an exceptional wrist spinner who used his brain as well as his skill to get the better of batsmen.

FOR THE RECORD

Brian Close was born at Rawdon, Yorkshire, on 24 February 1931. In 22 Tests he scored 887 runs and took 18 wickets. In his first season with Yorkshire in 1949 and at the age of 18, Brian completed the double of 1,000 runs and 100 wickets. At 18 years, 149 days, he became England's youngest ever Test player. His best bowling analysis was eight for 41 for Yorkshire against Kent in 1959. A fine all-rounder, his highest score was 198 for Yorkshire against Surrey at the Oval in 1960. He briefly played professional football with Leeds, Arsenal and Bradford City and is a single-handicap golfer whether playing right- or left-handed! During his career in which he was famed and feared for his competitive spirit, he captained Yorkshire, Somerset and England and was rated one of the great short-leg fielders.

DENIS COMPTON
Middlesex (1936–64)

MY CHILDHOOD BATTING HERO
The one and only Sir Jack Hobbs. My favourite treat when I was a lad was to be taken to Kennington Oval by my father to watch the great man in action. I used to study him through my father's field glasses and would marvel at his stroke play. He had a shot for every occasion. I was also a great admirer of his Surrey opening partner Andrew Sandham.

MY CHILDHOOD BOWLING HERO
Harold Larwood. Great pace was his prime weapon but he also kept an excellent line and length. I had the thrill of playing against Larwood and his partner Bill Voce in my second appearance for Middlesex.

MY IDEA OF THE PERFECT BATSMAN
Garfield Sobers and Graeme Pollock, both of whom were superb with the timing of their shots. Pollock had the gift of being equally strong on both front and back foot. Like all the great batsmen, his placing of shots was deadly

accurate and he could find gaps in the tightest fields. Sobers was, of course, the perfect all-rounder. His strength as a batsman was that he could turn a match with awesome attacking shots. Both Pollock and Sobers were adventurous players and both were left-handed batsmen.

MY IDEA OF THE PERFECT BOWLER

Ray Lindwall and Keith Miller, my old Australian adversaries. Both had beautiful actions to go with their natural flair.

FOR THE RECORD

Denis Compton was born in Hendon, Middlesex, on 23 May 1918. In 78 Tests he scored 5,807 runs at an average 50.06. During his career he totalled 38,942 runs, including 123 centuries. He made more than 1,000 runs in a season 17 times but it was one particular year – 1947 – when he cemented his place in the record books. In that magical summer of '47 he scored 3,816 runs at an average 90.85, completed a record 18 centuries and hammered 753 runs at an average 94.12 in five Tests against South Africa. He also found the time and energy to take 73 wickets with his slow, left-arm bowling that included a 'chinaman' as a bewildering speciality. He and his Middlesex and England team-mate Bill Edrich became known as the 'Terrible Twins' because of their long-running partnership. In the second half of his career he was handicapped by a knee injury collected while playing football with distinction as a left winger for Arsenal.

COLIN COWDREY
Kent (1950–75)

MY CHILDHOOD BATTING HERO
Denis Compton. It was as much his attitude as his brilliantly inventive batting that appealed to me. He was always entertaining as well as enterprising and inspired a whole generation of young cricketers.

MY CHILDHOOD BOWLING HERO
Douglas Wright. He had leg spin bowling down to a fine art, making the ball turn and lift and deceiving even the greatest batsmen with his clever flight and deceptive pace. I had the pleasure of taking my first catch for Kent off his bowling.

MY IDEA OF THE PERFECT BATSMAN
I have to give equal rating to Jack Hobbs, Walter Hammond, Peter May, Garfield Sobers, Vivian Richards and Frank Worrell. None were too 'professional' in their approach. They were all masters but cheerful, serene, able to smile and radiate pleasure while accumulating their runs.

MY IDEA OF THE PERFECT BOWLER
Brian Statham. A captain's dream who would bowl at any end, any time and in any conditions, always putting the team first. He never argued with umpires, the opposition, the crowd or colleagues who may have dropped catches off his bowling. He was a wonderful servant to Lancashire and England and always represented cricket with dignity.

FOR THE RECORD

See page 51

WILLIE RUSHTON'S
DREAM TEAM

1 DR W. G. GRACE *(capt)*
2 COLIN MILBURN
3 VIV RICHARDS
4 DENIS COMPTON
5 KEITH MILLER
6 SIR LEARIE CONSTANTINE
7 GODFREY EVANS
8 RAY LINDWALL
9 FRED TRUEMAN
10 JIM LAKER
11 JACK IVERSON

'W.G. is there because I've written a novel about him (It's called *W.G. Grace's Last Case*, is published by Methuen and is a sequel to *War of the Worlds!*). The rest of the side are all heroes of mine. I saw them all play with the exception of Australian spin wizard Jack Iverson, whom I sense is one bowler capable of going through anyone else's Dream Team. The great Learie Constantine I once fielded alongside in the slips for the old Rothmans Cavaliers. I never saw the snick he so generously knocked in the air in my direction with a charming call of "Yours!" The rest speak for themselves, all crowd-pleasers in their own way. Of course, there are omissions. I anticipate a terse note from Sir Donald but I only ever saw him once and he was out second ball. With each at the height of his powers, on song and playing on a perfect summer's day I'd back my lot against all comers. My twelfth man would be Derek Randall, the Last Great Character of cricket. The splendid Tom Graveney? Sorry, he's in the Second XI which will appear in the sequel to this book!

WILLIE RUSHTON

WILLIE RUSHTON, actor, writer, comedian, illustrator, satirical cartoonist, co-founder of *Private Eye* and general man-about-town genius, is a cricket fanatic and a keen Lord's Taverner. He learned the basics of the game at Shrewsbury School and nowadays, bearded and distinguished, delights in being mistaken for the great W.G. Grace. Bowlers always say Grace when he comes to the wicket . . . because they are about to make a meal of him!

MIKE DENNESS
Kent and Essex (1959–80)

MY CHILDHOOD BATTING HERO
Peter May. Living in Scotland, I got few opportunities to watch live first-class cricket but I saw enough on television to appreciate that May was the *complete* batsman. I tried to model myself on his application and style.

MY CHILDHOOD BOWLING HERO
I had eyes only for the batsmen but the bowler who came across as being both exciting and effective was Fred Trueman. He had personality to go with his ability.

MY IDEA OF THE PERFECT BATSMAN
It has to be Peter May. He was always in control of the bowling, was elegant and had a marvellous temperament. His driving to mid-on and mid-off was a sheer joy to behold.

MY IDEA OF THE PERFECT BOWLER
Dennis Lillee – and I speak from hair-raising experience! On that 1974–75 tour he was tremendously quick and

hostile and since his back injury has learned to make full use of the ball, varying his pace and direction.

FOR THE RECORD

Mike Denness was born in Belshill, Lanarkshire, on 1 December 1940. He played in 28 Tests for England, 19 of them as captain, and scored 1,669 runs at an average 39.69. He was an outstanding captain with a good tactical brain and exceptional fielding ability that inspired his team-mates. He led Kent to three John Player League titles, the Benson & Hedges Cup twice and the Gillette Cup once. An attractive, hard-hitting batsman, he has since passed on his wealth of knowledge to the youngsters of Essex where he was the Second XI skipper.

TED DEXTER
Sussex (1956–68)

MY CHILDHOOD BATTING HERO
Len Hutton fired my imagination when I was a young lad with his batting performances. I have warm recollections of the first bat I ever owned. It was an autographed Len Hutton size 3, treble spring which I cleaned and oiled with all the loving care of a young girl tending her first pony. Hutton had excellent technique and a wide repertoire of strokes.

MY CHILDHOOD BOWLING HERO
Keith Miller always appealed to me with his cavalier approach. He was a fine all-rounder and when I was first taking a close interest in the game it was he and Ray Lindwall who were the scourge of English batsmen.

MY IDEA OF THE PERFECT BATSMAN
Sir Jack Hobbs must come closest to fitting the description of the 'perfect batsman'. In the films that I have seen of him in action he always looked so cool and poised and obviously found the whole thing simple. Everything I have ever read and heard about this legendary figure leads me to believe that by not seeing him in his prime I was deprived of a unique experience.

MY IDEA OF THE PERFECT BOWLER
Alan Davidson, Australia's left-arm opening bowler, had the finest action I have seen. He had the vital ingredients of movement, speed, control and accuracy all in one and was a delight to watch.

FOR THE RECORD

See page 36

BILL EDRICH
Norfolk and Middlesex (1934–58)

MY CHILDHOOD BATTING HERO
Ernest Tyldesley, elegant right-handed Lancashire and England batsman who reached 1,000 runs in a season 19 times. I admired him from afar because, living in Norfolk, I never saw him play but it was his score I always looked for first in the newspapers and he rarely let me down.

MY CHILDHOOD BOWLING HERO
Maurice Tate, the marvellous Sussex medium-pacer who could bowl all varieties. I have early memories of his deeds for Sussex and Tom Webster's cartoons of his big boots! He was great-hearted in everything he did.

MY IDEA OF THE PERFECT BATSMAN

Jack Hobbs, the batsman for *all* occasions. He could score runs on any pitch and in any conditions. He was also a great *man* who was always ready to help and encourage young players.

MY IDEA OF THE PERFECT BOWLER

Ray Lindwall, a great friend and adversary who could swing the ball either way, could vary his pace and direction and who was exceptionally quick.

FOR THE RECORD

Bill Edrich was born at Lingwood, Norfolk, on 26 March 1916. He scored 86 centuries, including six in 39 Tests. He had his greatest season in harness with his Middlesex and England 'twin' Denis Compton in 1947. Edrich scored 3,539 runs at an average 80.43 with 12 centuries and also took 67 wickets with his enthusiastic pace bowling. He was at the opposite end in 1953 when his partner and pal Compton hit the winning run to regain the Ashes at The Oval. A good-class right winger, he played professional football for Norwich and Spurs. Three of his brothers also played County cricket and he is the cousin of John Edrich. A fighter on and off the pitch, he was awarded the DFC for wartime bombing raids over Germany.

BOBBY MOORE'S
DREAM TEAM

1 EVERTON WEEKES
2 FRANK WORRELL
3 VIV RICHARDS
4 GARFIELD SOBERS
5 IAN BOTHAM

6 KEITH MILLER
7 RAY LINDWALL
8 GODFREY EVANS
9 JIM LAKER
10 ALEC BEDSER
11 WES HALL

'While this is a dream team on paper it would have been a nightmare for any side having to play against them! Imagine getting rid of Weekes, Worrell and Viv Richards and then seeing Garry Sobers still at the wicket, with Ian Botham walking in to join him. The middle order's not bad either, with Keith Miller and Ray Lindwall there to give it a blast if necessary. Mind you, I can't believe that they would be needed with the four magnificent West Indian batsmen ahead of them. Lindwall and Hall would share the new ball, with Bedser and Miller coming on as change bowlers. Then Botham and Sobers can come in as a third wave, with Jim Laker waiting in the wings to baffle the batsmen with his spin.'

BOBBY MOORE

BOBBY MOORE, capped a record 108 times as an England footballer, was a County-class cricketer but chose to follow the big-ball game instead. He skippered England 90 times and led them to a memorable World Cup triumph in 1966. A magnificent defender with West Ham United and Fulham, he is now back in the game he served so well as manager of Southend United.

JOHN EDRICH
Surrey (1959–78)

MY CHILDHOOD BATTING HERO
Len Hutton. I used to follow his career closely but managed to see him play in the flesh only once . . . and he was out for nought and then one! Despite that disappointment, he remained my hero and I dreamt of one day following in his footsteps as an England opener.

MY CHILDHOOD BOWLING HERO
Ray Lindwall. I never got to see him play but used to listen to his exploits on the radio. It was a great thrill for me to meet him in the flesh on my first Australian tour. I know from speaking to his old team-mates and opponents that he used to generate tremendous speed and he could move the ball in the air or off the pitch.

MY IDEA OF THE PERFECT BATSMAN
Of all the greatest batsmen I have played with or against, Peter May left the biggest impression. He always seemed to get himself in the right position to make his shots and would really dominate the bowlers.

MY IDEA OF THE PERFECT BOWLER
Dennis Lillee is a young fast bowler's dream. He has pace, direction, wonderful action and can make the ball move either way. He also has a great change of pace that can deceive batsmen.

FOR THE RECORD
John Edrich was born at Bloefield, Norfolk, on 21 June 1937. He scored 103 centuries including 12 in 77 Tests. One of the greatest left-handed batsmen of all time, he amassed 1,799 runs for Surrey in his first season and topped 1,000 runs in a season 21 times. His most successful year was 1962 when he scored 2,482 runs at an average 51.71. On his Test debut against Australia at

Lord's in 1962 he carved out a century. He is the cousin of Bill Edrich and has been an England selector.

GODFREY EVANS
Kent (1939–59)

MY CHILDHOOD WICKET-KEEPING HERO
Leslie Ames, particularly when keeping wicket to Tich Freeman. They had a marvellous understanding and claimed many victims together. I used to watch Leslie play for Kent at every opportunity and apart from his wicket-keeping I also admired his batting. His policy of advancing down the wicket when batting earned him the nickname 'Twinkletoes'. He was a marvellous mentor and guide to me when I had the honour of following him into the Kent and England teams.

MY CHILDHOOD BATTING HERO
Wally Hammond, who was as good an all-round batsman as I've ever seen. He had a good technique, a sound defence and was a tremendous attacking player, particularly with his ferocious cover driving. When I grew up I had the pleasure and privilege of playing for England under his thoughtful captaincy.

MY IDEA OF THE PERFECT BOWLER
Ray Lindwall for variation of pace . . . Doug Wright for sheer brilliance . . . Alec Bedser for being a tiger who never stopped trying.

MY IDEA OF THE PERFECT BATSMAN
Denis Compton for his sheer genius . . . Len Hutton for correctness in style . . . Don Bradman for concentration.

MY IDEA OF THE PERFECT WICKET-KEEPER
The Australian Don Tallon, whose reactions were incredibly quick. (For Godfrey's Top Ten Wicket-Keepers, see page 00.)

FOR THE RECORD

See page 27

KEITH FLETCHER
Essex (1962–   )

MY CHILDHOOD BATTING HERO
I lived in Cambridgeshire as a youngster and did not get the opportunity to see much County cricket. But I followed it avidly on radio, TV and in the newspapers and the batsman whose scores I always looked for first was Peter May. There was an elegance and mastery about his play that appealed to me.

MY CHILDHOOD BOWLING HERO
I was 12 years old when Jim Laker produced his incredible 19-wicket performance against the Australians at Old Trafford in 1956 and like so many schoolboys I became an instant fan of his. It has to be the most devastating bowling display of all time. I had the pleasure of playing with Jim when he wound down his distinguished career with Essex.

MY IDEA OF THE PERFECT BATSMAN
For the big occasion, I would have to select Garry Sobers. He always saved his greatest performances for the Test

stage. The finest right-handed batsmen that I have played against are Barry Richards and Greg Chappell.

MY IDEA OF THE PERFECT BOWLER
Dennis Lillee and Freddie Trueman are the closest to perfection that I have seen. Both were exceptionally quick and had the ability to make the ball swing either way.

FOR THE RECORD

Keith Fletcher was born in Worcester on 20 May 1944. He has scored more than 30,000 runs, has captained England and has been the most successful skipper in Essex cricketing history. He led Essex to their first major triumphs in 1979 and is acknowledged as one of the best tacticians on the County circuit. Known to his team-mates as 'Gnome', he scored two centuries in a match against Notts at Trent Bridge in 1976. His highest score was an unbeaten 228 for Essex against Sussex at Hastings in 1968 and he once took five for 51 with his leg breaks against Middlesex at Colchester.

MIKE GATTING
Middlesex (1975–)

MY CHILDHOOD BATTING HERO
Basil D'Oliveira. He had a beautifully relaxed, natural way of facing even the most hostile bowling and was always a credit to cricket both on and off the pitch. He played with an aggressive yet graceful style that meant he was always worth watching.

MY CHILDHOOD BOWLING HERO
John Snow. He was a great competitor as well as having good pace and direction. He produced some marvellous

bowling performances, particularly in Australia in 1970–71 when his 31 wickets played a big part in our regaining of the Ashes.

MY IDEA OF THE PERFECT BATSMAN

Kenny Barrington, for so many reasons – his never-give-up spirit, his ability to adjust his game to any situation, his courage, concentration and his unselfish manner. Wally Grout best summed up his approach to an England crisis situation when he said he seemed to have a Union Jack trailing behind him when he walked to the wicket.

MY IDEA OF THE PERFECT BOWLER

Dennis Lillee, for guts, determination, movement of the ball, deadly accurate line and length and his ability to bowl a side out on good batting wickets. You can't help but admire him for the way he came back after a back injury to bowl as well if not better, varying his pace and his direction. A great competitor.

FOR THE RECORD

Mike Gatting was born in Kingsbury, Middlesex, on 6 June 1957. He is a fine all-round sportsman who chose a career in cricket rather than in football. His brother, Steve, started his professional football career with Arsenal and played for Brighton in the 1983 FA Cup Final. Mike is also accomplished at golf, table tennis, lawn tennis and swimming. As well as being a positive, hard-hitting batsman, he is also a good-class medium-pace bowler. He graduated from the England schools side that toured the West Indies in 1976. After some inconsistent performances he was dropped from the England team but was recalled for the 1984–5 tour to India. He responded with an avalanche of runs, including his first Test century in the Madras match. Mike is captain of Middlesex and was vice-captain of England in India.

SUNIL GAVASKAR
Bombay and India (1966–)

MY CHILDHOOD HERO
Only batsmen took my eye as a youngster. It never occurred to me to take too much notice of the bowlers. I was too busy studying the technique and styles of various batsmen. One player stood out for me above all others and that was West Indian right-handed batsman Rohan Kanhai. I remember that he had a particularly oustanding tour of India in 1958–59 when I was an impressionable schoolboy. He scored 538 runs in five Tests against India, including a splendid 256 at Calcutta. From then on I was a Rohan Kanhai fan.

MY IDEA OF THE PERFECT BOWLER
Bishen Singh Bedi, India's master of slow left-arm orthodox bowling, is the cricketing genius who comes nearest to fitting that description of being perfect. He had a smooth, easy run-up, a lovely action and follow-through and all the guile in the world. Bishen turned spin bowling into an art form. He could vary his pace, his flight, the degree of spin and the height at which the ball would come off the pitch. In a six-ball over he could deliver six totally different types of spin, completely baffling the batsman with his sleight of hand. He had limitless stamina and was a captain's delight in that he was willing to bowl all day if necessary.

MY IDEA OF THE PERFECT BATSMAN
I must stick with my boyhood hero Rohan Kanhai. He had a nice relaxed stance, a solid defence and all the strokes in the book plus some of his own. He made many bowlers all over the world suffer, particularly with his devastating sweep to leg that brought him boundaries galore. I had the pleasure of playing against him in the 1970–71 Test series in the West Indies when I made my debut for India. I really enjoyed getting a close-up view of the batsman whom I had admired for so long and I was not disappoin-

ted. He had real class and could dominate any attack
when in top form.

FOR THE RECORD

Sunil Gavaskar was born in Bombay on 10 July 1949. He has
become the greatest gatherer of Test runs in cricket history,
overtaking the one and only Sir Donald Bradman during the
1983 series against the West Indies. Typical of his modesty, he
was quick to point out that Bradman had reached his run record
in far fewer Tests (see Top Ten Statistics section). Despite
standing just under 5ft 5in, Gavaskar is a master at playing pace
bowling and he continually lays solid foundations to the Indian
innings as a dominating opening batsman who builds his monster
scores from a springboard of a technically perfect defence. While
it is his defence that first takes the eye, his strokeplay then
demands attention after he has seen the shine off the new ball.
He has a wide range of shots, specialising in powerful drives,
precision-placed cuts and delicate glances. Cricket is all-consum-
ing for this likeable little man who brings the sort of concentration to the wicket that would do justice to a chess master. When
the editor of the *Book of Cricket Lists* asked him what he liked to
do away from the cricket field, he replied: 'Think about cricket.'

GRAHAM GOOCH
Essex (1973–)

MY CHILDHOOD BATTING HERO
Keith Fletcher. I always used to look forward to seeing
him bat for Essex at my local grounds in Ilford and
Leyton. He was a player of the highest quality and now
that I have the pleasure of playing under him in the Essex
team I can vouch for the fact that he is maintaining that
standard. Keith has excellent technique and has the ability

to adapt his batting to the needs of the team. And with Keith, the team priorities always come first.

MY CHILDHOOD BOWLING HERO
Fred Trueman. He was a real character and one of the great fast bowlers who had the ability to swing the ball at high speed. Fred was also very competitive, of course, which added an extra edge to his game. To my young eyes he looked a giant out there on the field and he used to generate tremendous excitement as he thundered in to bowl.

MY IDEA OF THE PERFECT BATSMAN
Barry Richards is without question the best batsman I've played against. He had all the shots and made batting look easy. His timing was perfect and he had power and precision all round the wicket, often showing great invention when a scoring shot just didn't seem on. It was a pleasure to watch him in action, even when having to chase his shots to the boundary.

MY IDEA OF THE PERFECT BOWLER
Mike Procter, who was a truly aggressive fast bowler with the ability to bowl devastating in-swingers around the wicket. He was deadly accurate as well, which is reflected in the fact that he has taken four hat-tricks. On a fast wicket, he was almost unplayable and he could also get bounce and life out of the most docile of tracks.

FOR THE RECORD

Graham Gooch was born at Leytonstone on 23 July 1953. He scored 1,861 runs in 30 Tests before his controversial ban from the Test arena for joining the rebel tour to South Africa. As well as being a powerful opening bat, he is also a useful medium-pace bowler who has broken many stubborn partnerships with his deceptive swing. He had the character and determination to overcome the batsman's most dreaded nightmare: a pair in his first Test match. He collected his double duck against the

Australians at Edgbaston in 1975 but his performances against the hostile West Indian pace attack on the 1980–81 tour underlined his arrival as an opener worthy of comparison with the greats of the game. It was his majestic innings of 120 for Essex against Surrey in the 1979 Benson & Hedges Final at Lord's that convinced the cricket world that here was a player of superstar quality.

DAVID GOWER
Leicestershire (1975–   )

MY CHILDHOOD BATTING HERO
Graeme Pollock was one of my earlier idols. I saw him in a Test match at Trent Bridge and later in a game in Port Elizabeth. He scored a hundred each time and cemented my appreciation of him. Another left-hander who made a big impression on me – and on just about everybody who ever saw him – was Garfield Sobers. One day at Trent Bridge I saw him destroy an attack with 77 runs in about 40 minutes. It was magnificent stuff and I felt privileged to be a spectator.

MY CHILDHOOD BOWLING HERO
John Snow was the man who used to take my eye as a youngster. I liked his approach to the game. He was very competitive and aggressive and you always felt something was about to happen when he ran in to bowl.

MY IDEA OF THE PERFECT BATSMAN
Greg Chappell, who combines good technique with good temperament and plenty of shots. He is a classical front-foot player and always looks in command of the situation whenever he is at the wicket. He is never frightened to go for his shots and is a fine hooker of the ball.

MY IDEA OF THE PERFECT BOWLER

Of recent times, Dennis Lillee must come as close as any. He has pace, control, good bowling sense; all contribute to his overall effect. He is a showman who always gives spectators value for money and he is also a man of courage as he has proved by overcoming a back injury that threatened his career as a Test bowler. His record haul of Test wickets is a lasting testimony to his talent. Of the spinners, Derek Underwood, Bishen Bedi and John Emburey all have great control and variety.

FOR THE RECORD

See page 24

TOM GRAVENEY
Gloucestershire and Worcester (1948–71)

MY CHILDHOOD BATTING HERO

Wally Hammond was the master batsman who used to get me excited as a youngster. There have been few, if any, better exponents of the batting arts. He was a majestic sight when in full flow. I used to consider it worth the admission money just to see him walk out to the wicket.

MY CHILDHOOD BOWLING HERO

I was more in to watching the batsmen at work but the two bowlers whose performances excited me most of all were Yorkshire spinner Hedley Verity and Essex fast bowler Ken Farnes. Verity was a left-arm spinner in the classical mould, often delivering at medium pace and baffling batsmen with his flight and spin. Farnes, who stood 6ft

5in, generated tremendous speed off a run-up of just 11 paces.

MY IDEA OF THE PERFECT BATSMAN

Peter May, who was a disciplined, superb stroke player and a big-innings man with tremendous power all round the wicket. He was a player youngsters could learn from as opposed to the unorthodox genius of Denis Compton who used to weave a magic of his own that no coach could possibly pass on to a pupil.

MY IDEA OF THE PERFECT BOWLER

For speed, Ray Lindwall who could generate tremendous pace but without losing his line and length. For spin, Jim Laker who was a complete master of his art. Both Lindwall and Laker were strong competitive players but without losing sight of the fact that cricket is a game to be enjoyed.

FOR THE RECORD

Tom Graveney was born at Riding Mill, Northumberland, on 16 June 1927. He scored 122 centuries including 11 in 79 Tests. He topped 1,000 runs in a season 21 times and was the first batsman to score a ton of tons in post-war cricket. A master off his front foot, he scored two centuries in a match on four occasions. He was a great favourite in Australia where he lived for a spell while serving Queensland as player-coach. His highest Test score was 258 for England against the West Indies at Trent Bridge in 1957. He shared a record fourth wicket stand of 402 with Willie Watson when playing for the MCC against British Guyana in 1953–54. His contribution was 231. A thoughtful tactician, he captained Gloucester, Worcester and England. He is a single-handicap golfer and is a respected member of the BBC-TV cricket team.

KIM HUGHES
Western Australia (1975–   )

MY CHILDHOOD HERO
I lived deep in the country as a boy and so I had to rely on cricket books to fire my imagination. The books in our local library all featured pre-war stars and the player I never tired of reading about was Don Bradman. His feats with the bat were extraordinary to the point of being freakish. I just wish I had seen him play because he must have been a complete master of the game. His career average of 95.14 was just unbelievable and to have scored at an average 99.94 in Tests is lasting evidence that he was a quite exceptional batsman. He is a legendary figure of the game and he was my hero when I was a schoolboy even though I was not born until five years after his retirement.

MY IDEA OF THE PERFECT BATSMAN
To be perfect you would need to have the technique, concentration and competitive qualities of a Geoff Boycott and the power, grace and dashing strokeplay of a Viv Richards. The player who had a mixture of all those qualities is Barry Richards. He managed to make it all look so easy, stroking the ball to the boundary with effortless shots that were perfectly placed and beautifully timed. In Australia, cricket followers still recall the match in 1971 when he scored 325 runs in a day for South Australia against Western Australia at Perth. He totalled 1,538 runs that season at an average 109.86. That was batting in the Bradman class.

MY IDEA OF THE PERFECT BOWLER
Imran Khan comes closest to being the perfect bowler. He has strength and stamina to go with his speed and is the sort of great competitor who can produce his best when it is most needed. He is at his most effective and dangerous with a ball that has lost its shine and he has the ability to

produce prodigious swing in almost any conditions. A match can never be considered won when Imran is in opposition because, whether batting or bowling, he will keep trying until the final ball to turn the game in Pakistan's favour.

FOR THE RECORD

Kimberley John Hughes was born in Western Australia on 26 January (appropriately Australia Day) in 1954. Growing up in the country outside Perth, he developed his own natural ability as a brilliant schoolboy player and has retained it throughout his senior career. As a batsman he is a delight to the eye, always going for his shots and displaying a wide repertoire of strokes that are executed with flair and style. He is also a fine all-round fielder with a safe pair of hands and razor-sharp reflexes. Modest and with a pleasant personality, he became Australian Test captain at the age of 25 after just ten Tests. Nobody who saw him in action in the Centenary Test at Lord's in 1980 is likely to forget his two knocks against England. His 117 in the first innings was spread over three rain-interrupted days and contained a flow of superb shots despite the continual stoppages that would have destroyed the concentration and rhythm of most batsmen. In his second innings he rushed to 84 in 114 minutes, including three sixes and 14 fours in a breath-taking display of savage yet controlled batting. There are few better sights in modern cricket than Kim Hughes in full flow. The tears he shed when standing down as Australian captain in 1984 provided dramatic evidence of how much he cares about his cricket and his country.

SIR LEN HUTTON
Yorkshire (1934–60)

MY CHILDHOOD BATTING HERO
Jack Hobbs and Herbert Sutcliffe were the England batsmen whose exploits used to make me excited when I

was a lad. Hobbs in particular was a favourite of mine because he made everything seen so simple yet was a classical player. He and my Yorkshire hero Herbert Sutcliffe were magnificent opening partners for England, balancing each other perfectly and giving the team the strongest possible foundation.

MY CHILDHOOD BOWLING HERO

Wilfred Rhodes was a remarkably gifted all-rounder for Yorkshire and England. A forceful right-hand bat, he could bemuse the best batsmen with his subtle slow left-arm spin and flight. He would have walked into any team on his bowling alone but was also one of the best batsmen of his era, scoring more than 2,000 runs for England in 58 Tests.

MY IDEA OF THE PERFECT BATSMAN

Walter Hammond – and I speak with the advantage of often having been at the other wicket watching him in smooth, elegant action. I learned a lot from playing with him. He was a genius who could play every stroke in the book. The fact that he hit six Test double centuries speaks volumes for his great powers of concentration.

MY IDEA OF THE PERFECT BOWLER

The two that I select from the many I was lucky to play with and against are Hedley Verity and Keith Miller. Both were as near perfect as you can get, not only with their ability but also with their approach to the game. Both were outstanding sportsmen who always played with total enthusiasm. Verity followed in the great Yorkshire tradition of Peate, Peel and Rhodes – all of them brilliant left-arm spin bowlers. He was just about unplayable at times and he twice took ten wickets in an innings to prove it. Miller was the perfect foil for Ray Lindwall. He was not the fastest bowler by any means but you never knew what to expect because no two balls were the same. His unpredictability made him really difficult to bat against.

FOR THE RECORD

Sir Len Hutton was born in Pudsey, Yorkshire, on 23 June 1916. He scored 40,140 runs at an average 55.51 during a career that stretched from 1934 to 1960. He scored 129 centuries, including 19 in Test matches. Sir Len's innings of 364 for England against Australia at The Oval in 1938 was a world record Test haul that stood for nearly 30 years. He was the first professional cricketer to be appointed England captain on a long-term basis and never lost a rubber in 23 Test matches as skipper. A prolific run maker for Yorkshire throughout his career, he followed Sir Jack Hobbs as the second England cricketer to be honoured with a knighthood.

RAY ILLINGWORTH
Yorkshire and Leicestershire (1951–82)

MY CHILDHOOD BOWLING HERO
I was in my teens when I first became aware of Australian pace bowler Ray Lindwall. When I first saw him in action I thought he was the best fast bowler I had seen and I have not come across a better one since.

MY CHILDHOOD BATTING HERO
Len Hutton was every Yorkshire schoolboy's hero in my generation and I was no different. I was just six years old when he first captured everybody's attention with his magnificent 364 for England against Australia at The Oval. Who would have dreamt that thirteen years later I would be playing alongside him in the Yorkshire team?

MY IDEA OF THE PERFECT BOWLER
Ray Lindwall remains the closest I have seen to perfection. He had a perfect action and was intelligent with his variation of pace and strength.

MY IDEA OF THE PERFECT BATSMAN

I stick with my boyhood hero, Len Hutton. He was the complete batsman on all wickets. He had excellent technique and he never used to let anything interfere with his concentration. His discipline and determination were a lesson to all cricketers.

FOR THE RECORD

Ray Illingworth, like the great Len Hutton, was born in Pudsey, on 8 June 1932. Recognised as one of the game's greatest tacticians, he skippered Leicestershire and England before returning to Yorkshire as team manager and occasional player. He took 122 wickets and scored 1,836 runs in 61 Tests. An intelligent and cunning spin bowler, he took 100 wickets in a season ten times and also scored 1,000 runs in a season eight times. To underline his standing as a top-flight all-rounder he did the 100 wickets, 1,000 runs double on six occasions. His best Test bowling return was six for 29 against India at Lord's in 1967 and his highest Test score was 113 against the West Indies at Lord's in 1969. He left Yorkshire after eighteen years in 1969 to become captain of Leicestershire and shaped them into County champions. His leadership helped England regain the Ashes in Australia in 1971.

TREVOR HOWARD'S
DREAM TEAM

1 JACK HOBBS
2 FRANK WOOLLEY
3 DON BRADMAN
4 WALTER HAMMOND
5 DENIS COMPTON
6 GRAEME POLLOCK

7 **FRANK WORRELL** *(capt)*
8 **KEITH MILLER**
9 **ALAN DAVIDSON**
10 **RAY LINDWALL**
11 **GODFREY EVANS**

'It may seem churlish on Bradman that I have selected Worrell as skipper but the side is so strong in both batting and bowling that I don't think it really matters who is captain. It was sheer torture having to confine my selection to just eleven players and not being able to find room for players of the quality of Arthur Morris, Ponsford, Hassett, Oldfield, Sobers, Bedser, Sutcliffe, Verity . . . I could, of course, go on and on. In the end I have plumped for what I consider a finely balanced side, although I must admit I'm possibly weak in the spin department. If the "dream match" is to be played on a turning wicket, I'll call up Verity to replace Davidson. Verity and Woolley sharing the slow-bowling duties should have the batsmen in a spin!'

TREVOR HOWARD

TREVOR HOWARD, one of Britain's most distinguished actors, has had a life-long love affair with cricket. He is a member of the MCC and it has been known for him to have a clause written into his film contracts that he must be released for five days during any Lord's Test match!

IMRAN KHAN
Lahore, Worcestershire and Sussex (1969–   )

MY CHILDHOOD HERO
When I was a young boy growing up in Pakistan I considered cricket exclusively a batsman's game. I idolised both my cousins Majid Khan and Javed Burki. I had the thrill of seeing Javed score a fine century against the MCC at Lahore, while Majid produced many hurricane knocks at school and club level which left a lasting impression on me.

MY IDEA OF THE PERFECT BOWLER
Purely as far as the bowling action is concerned, I select Michael Holding. He has perfect rhythm and fluency. His high arm action and full utilisation of his height means he gets natural swing and off-the-pitch movement either way. He also gets steep bounce and added to all this is his immense speed. The only reason he has not been even more successful is because of injuries and also, in my view, because he has not worked hard enough at his bowling to get the absolute maximum out of his astonishing natural ability.

MY IDEA OF THE PERFECT BATSMAN
Vivian Richards is the batsman on whom the description 'perfect' sits quite comfortably. He can attack and defend at will and with an ease of movement and a ferocious yet controlled power that is admired even by the bowlers whose averages he ruins! Above all he plays fast bowling better than anybody else and always seems to have so much time to make his shots, which is the mark of an outstanding batsman. Along with all his other attributes, he also has an incredibly good big-match temperament.

FOR THE RECORD

Imran Khan was born at Lahore on 25 November 1952. One of

the world's finest all-round talents, he is a magnificent match-winning fast bowler and a batsman of great flair and style. He was seen at his best in the 1976–77 Test series against Australia, particularly in Sydney when his 12 wickets for 165 lifted Pakistan to their first Test victory in Australia. He has flourished his cricketing skills for Oxford University, Worcestershire and Sussex and his good looks and pleasant personality have made him almost as popular a performer in England as in his homeland. Wisden *voted* him one of their Cricketers of the Year in 1983 following his feats with the bat and the ball in the Test series against England during which his calculating captaincy, his devastating bowling and his suddenly matured batting all went to prove that he is now without question one of the world's most gifted cricketers.

SYED KIRMANI
Mysore (1967–   )

MY CHILDHOOD WICKET-KEEPING HERO
I idolised no wicket-keeper in particular but I was greatly inspired and assisted by both Alan Knott and Bob Taylor. I was fortunate to meet both of them and their tips and guidance were of immense help to me as I began to develop my game. Both Alan and Bob were very kind and courteous and were always willing to converse and share experiences. I have a lot of admiration for both of them, both as players and as people.

MY CHILDHOOD BATTING AND BOWLING HERO
It is one of the great regrets of my life that I never saw the great Sir Garfield Sobers at his peak. I admired him from afar when I was a youngster and would have loved to have seen him in action but it was not to be and I had to content myself with watching film of this extraordinarily gifted cricketer.

MY IDEA OF THE PERFECT WICKET-KEEPER

Bob Taylor is the wicket-keeper I would hold up as an example for every youngster coming into the game. He has a near copybook technique and his swift collections, agility and anticipation make him a joy to watch.

MY IDEA OF THE PERFECT BATSMAN

In my opinion Gundappa Viswanath comes nearest to being the perfect batsman. He can play every stroke in the book all round the wicket and with proper technique, grace and ease. He has strong yet supple wrists and strikes the ball with tremendous power but never at the expense of correct timing and touch.

FOR THE RECORD

Syed Kirmani was born in India on 29 December 1949. He is a good enough right-handed batsman to win a Test place for his batting alone but it is as a stylish wicket-keeper that he has established himself as a player respected throughout the cricketing world. A long-time understudy to Farokh Engineer, he made an instant impact when he finally got his chance to take his place behind the stumps in the 1975–76 series against New Zealand. In the second Test at Christchurch he equalled the Test record of six victims in an innings, holding five catches and stumping a sixth batsman. He scored his maiden Test century with an unbeaten 101 against Australia in Bombay in 1979–80 and contributed 67 runs to India's biggest ever total of 487 against England in the third Test at New Delhi in the 1981–82 series.

MICHAEL BENTINE'S
DREAM TEAM

1 DON BRADMAN
2 GEOFF BOYCOTT
3 RANJITSINHJI
4 DENIS COMPTON
5 FRANK WOOLLEY
6 PERCY CHAPMAN
7 MAURICE TATE
8 BILL O'REILLY
9 FREDDIE TRUEMAN
10 GEORGE DUCKWORTH
11 HAROLD LARWOOD

'My reasons for each selection is as follows – Bradman for his sheer style and grace; Boycott for guts and determination; Ranji because he was a batsman supreme; Compton because he is my ideal of a sportsman; Woolley for his heroic batting; Chapman because he was a great all-rounder; Tate, a big-hearted swing bowler and a free-hitting batsman; O'Reilly for spin bowling at its best; Trueman for fire and sheer value; Duckworth for reliability and skill behind the stumps; and Larwood, the daddy of all fast bowlers. None of these great cricketers ever gave less than their best and together I suggest they would make an unbeatable combination.'

MICHAEL BENTINE

MICHAEL BENTINE learned the qualities of cricket and cricketers on the playing fields of Eton before becoming a founder member of the Goons and one of the most inventive comedians and comedy writers in the world of entertainment.

ALAN KNOTT
Kent (1964–)

MY CHILDHOOD HEROES
My father was my big hero when I was a boy. He used to
play for Belvedere Cricket Club with my uncle, brother,
cousin and myself. Dad taught me the finer points of
cricket from the age of four and in the early days of my
career he kept wicket to my off-spin bowling. My batting
hero was Hampshire opener Roy Marshall and Freddie
Trueman was the bowler I used to love to watch.

MY IDEA OF THE PERFECT BATSMAN
It has to be Garry Sobers, who was always in command of
the situation with marvellous stroke play. It must have
been almost a privilege for bowlers to be taken apart by
him!

MY IDEA OF THE PERFECT BOWLER
Slow – Derek Underwood, a great bowler on all wickets
and just unplayable on any wicket giving him a little help.
Fast – Dennis Lillee, who never stops trying and can bowl
at pace all day long.

MY IDEA OF THE PERFECT WICKET-KEEPER
I only saw Godfrey Evans play 'live' after he had finished
his first-class career but he was still brilliant and I can't
imagine there has been anybody better than him at his
peak. If I had to pick a wicket-keeper from my era for a
world side it would be Rod Marsh. He is a magnificent
all-rounder, with gloves and bat. He and Dennis Lillee
have a great understanding and it's a treat to watch them
working together.

FOR THE RECORD

Alan Knott was born in Belvedere, Kent, on 9 April 1946. In 95
Tests he made 269 dismissals, holding 250 catches and stumping

19 victims. He was also a solid batsman, scoring 4,389 runs for England at an average 32.75. Voted Young Cricketer of the Year in 1965, he made his Test debut against Pakistan two years later and held seven catches. He held the record for most dismissals by a wicket-keeper in Test cricket until overtaken by Rodney Marsh. His highest Test score was 135 for England against Australia at Trent Bridge in 1977 and he scored two unbeaten centuries in a County match against Surrey in 1972. He runs a successful sports shop business in Herne Bay.

JIM LAKER
Surrey and Essex (1946–64)

MY CHILDHOOD BOWLING HERO
Hedley Verity, Yorkshire's wizard of spin whose left-arm deliveries could trick and trap the greatest of batsmen on the easiest of wickets. When I was just eight, I had a magical day out at Headingley when I watched him take his famous 10 wickets for 10 runs against Notts. The previous season he had taken 10 for 36 against Warwickshire on the same ground. He bowled only 52 balls against Notts and from that day on, of course, he was my big hero and I can honestly say that for the next nine years I cannot remember ever seeing him bowl badly. I treasure the memory of having been in his company shortly before he was killed while serving as a captain in the 8th Army in Sicily.

MY CHILDHOOD BATTING HERO
George Senior was the batsman who lit up my youth with a procession of adventurous knocks that provided marvellous entertainment. He was a balding Bradford League pro who dented the reputations of many overseas stars with his belligerent batting. Saturday afternoons could

never come quickly enough for me to watch him in thrilling action.

MY IDEA OF THE PERFECT BOWLER
If we're talking about speed, then it has to be Ray Lindwall who – in harness with Keith Miller – was a magnificent new ball bowler for Australia. He had great control in swing and movement and could produce a snorter from out of nowhere to unsettle the greatest of batsmen. If it's spin bowling, then the player I would select is Bishen Bedi. He coupled his spin with superb flight variations. Both Lindwall and Bedi had perfection in rhythm and action.

MY IDEA OF THE PERFECT BATSMAN
Sir Don Bradman is the most complete batsman I have ever seen. Concentration, technique, a full range of textbook shots plus several of his own making – the man had everything. His Test match average of 99.94 runs says all that needs to be said. He was a cricketing genius.

FOR THE RECORD

See page 31

DAVID LARTER
Northamptonshire (1960–67)

MY CHILDHOOD BOWLING HERO
Ray Lindwall. The visual spectacle of him in action – his rhythm, speed and swing – completely captivated me when I was at an impressionable age. Even when he was sending my England heroes back to the pavilion I didn't

mind too much because his bowling was something to be admired and envied.

MY CHILDHOOD BATTING HERO
I had two batsmen that I admired above all others – Denis Compton for sheer entertainment, invention and adventure and Len Hutton for application, technique and concentration. They were poles apart in their approach to cricket yet each in his own way was a master of the game and between them they gave hours of pleasure to cricket lovers the world over and were a credit to the England team.

MY IDEA OF THE PERFECT BOWLER
It has to be Fred Trueman. His action, attitude, temperament and stamina were ideal for the exacting job of bowling at speed against the best batsmen in the world. In his early days he was all fire but later in his career he developed into a very intelligent bowler, moving the ball either way and varying his pace so that the batsman did not know what to expect next.

MY IDEA OF THE PERFECT BATSMAN
Who else but the great Garfield Sobers? He had such fantastic natural ability that you could not bowl to him when he had made up his mind to get runs. He was powerful all round the batting compass and could pierce the tightest fields with perfectly placed shots. As an all-rounder, he was just untouchable.

FOR THE RECORD

David Larter was born in Inverness on 24 April 1940. He stood 6ft 7in, weighed 16 stone and for a spell was one of the world's most dynamic fast bowlers. His eventful career was sadly cut short by a succession of injuries after ten Test appearances in which he took 37 wickets at an average 25.43. His best career figures were eight for 28 against Somerset at Northampton in 1965. He went into business management after being forced into premature retirement at what should have been the peak of his career.

JOHN LEVER

Essex (1967–)

MY CHILDHOOD BOWLING HERO

Wes Hall. He started a new era in which bowlers became major crowd pullers instead of just the top run makers attracting all the publicity. He had a classical action and you always expected something to happen when he was on his powerful way in to bowl. Though tremendously fast he didn't let his line and length wander. He and Charlie Griffith in harness together for the West Indies were a chilling prospect for all batsmen.

MY CHILDHOOD BATTING HERO

Ted Dexter was the batsman whose approach to the game had most appeal for me. He always batted with style and flair and was never dull to watch. His policy was that the best form of defence is attack and it was a great spectacle to see him taking on the fast bowlers, driving with tremendous power off the front or back foot.

MY IDEA OF THE PERFECT BOWLER

Dennis Lillee. He is not just a very quick bowler but has fantastic control and can bowl with great effect on even the slowest wickets. I admire the way he has made a successful comeback after his back injury. He varies his direction and his pace and can lift his team-mates with the sheer force of his personality and his competitive nature. A great bloke to have on your side.

MY IDEA OF THE PERFECT BATSMAN

South African Barry Richards is the batsman who comes nearest to that description. He can play shots all around the wicket and has a sound technique. And like all the batting masters he has the quality of seeming to have time to pick up the line and length of the ball. He always looks in command at the wicket and is perfectly positioned to place his shots with what seems to be the least effort.

FOR THE RECORD

See page 45

TONY LEWIS
Glamorgan (1955–74)

MY CHILDHOOD BATTING HERO

Gilbert Parkhouse, the Glamorgan and England opening bat who exceeded 1,000 runs in a season 15 times. I admired him for his talent, his style and his art of movement. For Glamorgan, he shared many a long and delightful opening stand with Bernard Hedges and accumulated more than 23,000 runs during his career. He was also a first-rate slip field.

MY CHILDHOOD BOWLING HERO

J.C. (John) Clay, the Glamorgan and England right-arm slow bowler. He was a tall and distinguished amateur with a lovely action and he specialised in looping off-spinners. He gave his adopted County wonderful service and played a crucial role in Glamorgan's memorable first Championship triumph in 1948, later becoming President of the County and an England selector. He took 1,315 wickets at an average 19.77 and scored more than 7,000 runs as an enthusiastic tail-end batsman.

MY IDEA OF THE PERFECT BATSMAN
That description sits neatly on the shoulders of Tom Graveney. He had classical style, perfect timing and touch and a strength of purpose to dominate. It was a pleasure to watch his graceful batting and he radiated a feeling that he was at the wicket to enjoy himself, and this was a mood that spread to the spectators.

MY IDEA OF THE PERFECT BOWLER
F.S. (Fred) Trueman, for his great action and his ability to bowl a variety of balls at high speed. He was aggressive and very competitive but played a thinking man's game and had a deep understanding of the tactics of cricket.

FOR THE RECORD

Tony Lewis was born in Swansea on 6 July 1938. He captained Cambridge University, Glamorgan and England during a career in which he scored 20,495 runs at an average 32.42. He had his most prolific year in 1966 when he amassed 2,198 runs at an average 41.47. He was highly respected for his tactical knowledge and his inspiring leadership was a key point in Glamorgan's Championship victory in 1969. A Cricket and Rugby Blue at Oxford, he was a violinist with the National Youth Orchestra. He is now a regular broadcaster and cricket correspondent for the *Sunday Telegraph*.

DENNIS LILLEE
Western Australia (1969–)

MY CHILDHOOD BOWLING HERO
I had five favourites and I list them in no particular order: Ray Lindwall, Wes Hall, Alan Davidson, Freddie Trueman and Graham (Garth) McKenzie. They all appealed to me because of their speed, the determined way they played their cricket and because of the excitement they generated when running in to bowl. Wes Hall, in particular, had an influence on me and when I was a youngster first finding my feet as a fast bowler I used to imagine I was the giant West Indian as I ran in to bowl.

MY CHILDHOOD BATTING HERO
There were six batsmen that used to grab my attention: Colin Cowdrey, Rohan Kanhai, Ian Redpath, Garry Sobers, Bill Lawry and Ian Chappell. They were all special in their own way and each of them was able to dominate an attack when lesser batsmen would be struggling.

MY IDEA OF THE PERFECT BOWLER
Andy Roberts and John Snow get my vote in this category. At their peak, both have been magnificent fast bowlers able to vary their pace and direction and to make things happen on wickets that offered little assistance.

MY IDEA OF THE PERFECT BATSMAN
Greg Chappell, who has great composure to go with his stunning range of shots. He has the ability to master bowlers on bad wickets and can turn a game that seems lost with an innings of unmatched brilliance.

FOR THE RECORD

Dennis Lillee was born in Perth on 18 July 1949. He has virtually had two great careers as a fast bowler. The first was as a lightning-quick and aggressive new ball bowler who could devastate teams with the sheer pace of his deliveries. He established himself as a world-class pace-man in the 1972 Test series in England when he took 31 wickets, an Australian record. His career at the top seemed finished when stress fractures in his back temporarily forced him out of the game. But he fought his way back into the Australian firing line and, while lacking his early fearsome speed, he was even more deadly because of his uncanny accuracy and his ability to move the ball either way. There has rarely been anybody to match him as a determined competitor and the reward for his enormous effort is a world record haul of Test wickets (see 'Top Ten' Statistics section).

RODNEY MARSH
Western Australia (1968–   )

MY CHILDHOOD HEROES
Wally Grout was my wicket-keeping hero. Just the fact that he kept wicket for Australia was enough to make him No. 1 in my young eyes. My bowling heroes were Keith Miller and Ray Lindwall for pace and Richie Benaud for spin. The batsman I idolised was Neil Harvey, a cultured left-hander who took apart bowling attacks with the precision of a surgeon.

MY IDEA OF THE PERFECT WICKET-KEEPER
Alan Knott at his peak. He is brilliant standing back and has no equal when standing over the stumps. Knotty is far and away the best 'keeper of my era.

MY IDEA OF THE PERFECT BATSMAN
The perfect batsman would have the technique and skills of the Chappell brothers and the flair and brilliance of Viv and Barry Richards. Any batsman with that sort of combination would be classed as perfect.

MY IDEA OF THE PERFECT BOWLER

There is no question that the bowler who stands up to that description is D.K. (Dennis) Lillee. It has been a privilege for me to keep wicket to him for so long because he is the greatest bowler I have ever seen. He's got everything.

FOR THE RECORD

Rodney Marsh was born in Armadale, Western Australia, on 4 November 1947. He picked up the cruel nickname of 'Iron Gloves' early in his Test career because there were times when he failed to hold on to vital catches but he has long since silenced his critics and would now be more aptly named 'Golden Gloves'. He has claimed more victims than any wicket-keeper in Test match history and his partnership in Test and State cricket with Dennis Lillee has been one of the great features of the modern game. Marsh, whose brother, Graham, is one of the world's leading golfers, overtook his boyhood hero Wally Grout's 187-dismissals record in the 1977 Centenary Test against England in Melbourne. To make the match even more memorable, the belligerent left-hander became the first Australian wicket-keeper to score a century against England.

LESLIE CROWTHER'S
DREAM TEAM

1 GRAHAM GOOCH
2 BARRY RICHARDS
3 DAVID GOWER
4 VIV RICHARDS
5 DENIS COMPTON
6 TOM GRAVENEY
7 IAN BOTHAM
8 ALAN KNOTT

9 JIM LAKER
10 RAY LINDWALL
11 FREDDIE TRUEMAN

'Gooch, Barry and Viv Richards, Gower and Graveney epitomise the style and grace that makes cricket such a beautiful game – . . . Botham and Trueman are born winners . . . Compton is in so that I can sit and enjoy his grand sweep to leg . . . Knott is there for his gritty batting and brilliant wicket-keeping . . . Laker and Lindwall because there are no better bowlers than these two at the peak of their form. A rather select side, don't you think?'

LESLIE CROWTHER

LESLIE CROWTHER, comedy actor and television personality, is an enthusiastic and industrious Lord's Taverner who loves playing, watching and talking about the great game of cricket.

PETER MAY
Surrey (1948–63)

MY CHILDHOOD BATTING HERO
W. R. (Walter) Hammond, who scored 167 centuries to prove he had staying power to go with his immense natural talent. He had a classical style and the confidence and ability to play his shots on the most difficult wickets. He exceeded 1,000 runs in 22 seasons, including five times during overseas tours.

MY CHILDHOOD BOWLING HERO
Hedley Verity, who in his tragically short career proved himself one of the greatest of all left-arm spin bowlers. He

was an absolute terror to batsmen on a sticky wicket and also had the accuracy and pace and flight variations to cause problems on good batting surfaces.

MY IDEA OF THE PERFECT BATSMAN
Sir Jack Hobbs, with 197 centuries and more than 61,000 runs as evidence of his batting mastery. He was a model batsman who set a perfect example to young cricketers, not only with his poised and purposeful batting but also with his dignified and sporting approach to the game.

MY IDEA OF THE PERFECT BOWLER
Alec Bedser, who had the ability to produce match-winning performances on all wickets and in all conditions. He was a lion-hearted competitor who always put the needs of the team above any selfish considerations.

FOR THE RECORD

Peter May was born in Reading on 31 December 1929. He had a relatively short career in first-class competitive cricket but before he declared his innings over at the age of 32 he had established himself as one of the finest batsmen of all time, with a haul of 27,592 runs and a career average of 51.00. He first flourished his extraordinary batting skills at Charterhouse and then became a prolific run maker at Cambridge University where he also captained the soccer team. His greatest years were with Surrey whom he helped win seven successive County championships, the last two (1957/58) as captain. He was an inspiring captain of England for whom he averaged 46.77 in 66 Tests and he succeeded his old Surrey colleague Alec Bedser as chairman of the Test selectors.

COLIN MILBURN
Northamptonshire (1960–74)

MY CHILDHOOD BATTING HERO
I didn't have just one in particular but Colin Cowdrey, Denis Compton and Len Hutton were high on the list of batsmen that I admired. Cowdrey could stroke the ball to the boundary with what seemed effortless ease; Compton was full of the spirit of adventure and always had the spectators on the edge of their seats and the fielders on their toes; Hutton got his runs in painstaking fashion but had such good technique that he was never ever dull to watch.

MY CHILDHOOD BOWLING HERO
F. S. Trueman. And when Fred finds out, I'll never live it down! I loved his aggressive approach to the game and he had a good tactical brain to go with his brute force. If he failed to get a batsman out with sheer speed he would then try to *think* him out, varying his pace and direction and nagging away with a good line and length.

MY IDEA OF THE PERFECT BATSMAN
Garry Sobers was the best I ever saw. He regularly scored runs under pressure and had magnificent technique and a whole range of superb strokes that just came naturally to him. There was little a bowler could do to tie him down when he was in full flow apart from hope and pray that he would mis-hit. He could really swing the bat but was also capable of playing controlled, disciplined stuff if that was what the situation demanded.

MY IDEA OF THE PERFECT BOWLER
Derek Underwood, just about unplayable on an English 'turner' . . . Tom Cartwright and Derek Shackleton on an English seamer's wicket where their movement of the ball could make batting a nightmare . . . Wes Hall, the best fast bowler I faced on any wicket with speed that was quite

staggering . . . Fred Trueman, for the finest action and a competitive spirit that was never doused.

FOR THE RECORD

See page 39

DEREK SHACKLETON
Hampshire (1948–69)

MY CHILDHOOD HEROES
My boyhood cricket delight was watching Lancashire League cricket and I select two West Indian greats from that era, Learie Constantine and George Headley. Constantine played for Nelson and Headley for Hasingdon. Both were absolute masters of the game. Whether with the bat or the ball, Constantine had match-winning brilliance and was a marvel in the field where he turned potential boundaries into suicidal singles. He could be hostile when bowling flat out and could move the ball either way when concentrating on medium pace. Headley was a superb right-handed batsman who could dominate the best bowling attacks. Not for nothing was he known as the 'Black Bradman'. He had a solid defence but was at his scintillating best when playing his shots, particularly on the on side.

MY IDEA OF THE PERFECT BOWLER
F. S. (Fred) Trueman. He had the ideal build for a fast bowler, was very keen and aggressive without being malicious and it was always a pleasure to work at the other end as I did in the 1963 Test series against the West Indies. He was particularly devastating in the second and third

Tests, taking 11 wickets at Lord's and 12 at Edgbaston. I managed to get in on the act in the Lord's Test, taking three wickets in four balls to close the West Indies first innings. But Fred stole the show at Edgbaston with a stunning 24-ball spell in which he took the last six West Indies wickets at the cost of just one scoring shot which went for four. This was Fred at his fiery best.

MY IDEA OF THE PERFECT BATSMAN

Barry Richards, because he had a stroke for every ball and always had time to make his strokes. That's the art of great batmanship – making time to get in position and play the shots.

FOR THE RECORD

Derek Shackleton was born at Todmorden, Lancashire, on 12 August 1924. He gave an early indication of what was to become almost legendary consistency when in his first full season in County cricket in 1949 he missed the double of 100 wickets and 1,000 runs by only 86 runs. He set a remarkable record by taking 100 wickets in a season for 20 successive years. Only the great Wilfred Rhodes had bettered this, with 100 wickets a season 23 times. He was deadly accurate with his medium-fast seamers and had a career haul of 2,875 wickets at an average 18.65. Hampshire's man for all seasons, unlucky not to make more than seven appearances for England, was a useful right-hand bat who often produced down-the-order match-winning knocks.

FRANCIS MATTHEWS'
DREAM TEAM

1 LEN HUTTON
2 TOM GRAVENEY
3 DON BRADMAN
4 GARFIELD SOBERS
5 VIV RICHARDS
6 IAN BOTHAM
7 KEITH MILLER
8 RICHIE BENAUD
9 GODFREY EVANS
10 JIM LAKER
11 RAY LINDWALL

'The team is necessarily based on those I have spent many happy hours watching myself and points to the 1940s and 1950s apart from Richards and Botham. Tom Graveney's inclusion is not sycophancy! He and Len Hutton happen to be the most fluid, balanced and stylish of all the batsmen I have ever seen. The satisfaction of watching either of them build an innings from solid, watchful defence, through delicate deflections using the pace of the new ball and developing into those effortless, perfect cover drives of which they were both masters was to see what makes cricket the most beautiful of all games to watch. The rest of the team bats down to No. 9 and I have deliberately packed the middle order with the great all-rounders. As a Yorkshire-born fan who spent every spare summer moment at Headingley I was tempted to choose: Hutton, Sutcliffe, Watson, Boycott, Illingworth, Leyland, Yardley, Arthur Wood, Trueman, Bowes and Verity. Now that, by gum, is what you call a *dream* team!'

FRANCIS MATTHEWS

FRANCIS MATTHEWS, a fine actor who is perhaps best known for his portrayal of television's Paul Temple, is a cricket purist with a deep affection for the game he has watched since he was a youngster growing up in Yorkshire where the game was a way of life.

REG SIMPSON
Nottinghamshire (1944–63)

MY CHILDHOOD BATTING HERO
Sir Donald Bradman. He must still rank as one of the finest batsmen ever, if not *the* finest. He was a calculating craftsman who was also creative and his consistent run-making is lasting proof of his great powers of concentration and exceptional ability.

MY CHILDHOOD BOWLING HERO
Harold Larwood, who delivered the ball at tremendous speed at the end of what was a smooth, rhythmic run-up. His action was just about perfect. The pace he generated was never at the sacrifice of accuracy.

MY IDEA OF THE PERFECT BATSMAN
In this category would come batsmen who score large numbers of runs at a rate generally above average. Four who come easily to mind are Don Bradman, Denis Compton, Graeme Pollock and Garfield Sobers. All could dominate the bowlers and were capable of making their shots regardless of the pressure and the playing conditions.

MY IDEA OF THE PERFECT BOWLER
Ray Lindwall. He was a genuine fast bowler who could

move the ball both ways deliberately. His run up was smooth and economical and he had total control, developing a wicked in-swinger to go with his main delivery which was an out-swinger. He had amazing accuracy and seldom wasted a ball.

FOR THE RECORD

Reg Simpson was born in Sherwood, Nottinghamshire, on 27 February 1920. A master at handling hostile new ball bowling, he averaged 33.35 in 27 Tests and had a career aggregate of 30,546 runs. He scored 1,000 runs in a season 14 times and topped 2,500 runs on two occasions. His highest score was 259 for MCC against New South Wales in 1959 and his top score in England was an unbeaten 243 for Notts against Worcester at Trent Bridge in 1950. Notts captain from 1951 until 1960, he was a solid and dependable opening bat who was a superb striker of the ball and a top-class fielder.

MIKE SMITH
Leicestershire and Warwickshire (1951–75)

MY CHILDHOOD BATTING HERO
Denis Compton, who played with flair and style and was always exciting to watch. He did not always go by the book and it was his inventiveness and improvisation that was such an appealing part of his game. Although he made shots up as he went along, he was also very capable when it came to playing orthodox strokes – particularly the cover drive. But it was hooks, cuts and sweep shots that captured the imagination of a generation of school-boy cricket fans.

MY CHILDHOOD BOWLING HERO

Alec Bedser. He had enormous determination and a marvellous spirit to go with his ability. A master of medium-pace bowling, he could make the ball move either way and his leg cutter on broken or damp wickets was almost the equivalent of a fast leg break. He would be my choice as the 'perfect' bowler because he could be held up as an example to young cricketers for his technique, commitment and also his sportsmanship. He never gave anything less than 100 per cent for England and Surrey.

MY IDEA OF THE PERFECT BATSMAN

Rohan Kanhai, the West Indian maestro who was a player of the highest ability. He used to set out to dominate the opposition and was never frightened to go for his shots. It was my pleasure to play with him at Warwickshire and I never tired of watching him at the wicket where he was never dull or predictable. He was also a beautiful fielder, safe and reliable as slip or in the covers.

FOR THE RECORD

Mike Smith – known throughout the cricket world by his initials M. J. K. – was born in Broughton Astley, Leicestershire, on 30 June 1933. He was a brilliant all-rounder who was a double international, representing England at cricket and Rugby Union. He was a double Blue at Oxford, playing at fly-half in two Varsity matches at Twickenham and skippering the cricket team. Smith, who used to play in spectacles, played briefly for Leicestershire before joining Warwickshire where he became captain in 1957. In successive seasons between 1957 and 1962 he topped 2,000 runs and had his most prolific period in 1959 when he became the first batsman for ten years to exceed 3,000 runs. A magnificent short leg fielder, he scored 1,000 runs in a season 20 times and captained England 25 times in 50 Test appearances.

JOHN SNOW
Sussex and Warwickshire (1961–81)

MY CHILDHOOD HERO
Keith Miller. I fancied myself as an all-rounder and Keith was the player whose performances with the bat and ball really captured my imagination. He could communicate with the spectators, giving them entertainment while at the same time pouring every ounce of effort into his game. Whether he was holding the ball or the bat he was always exciting to watch. There was never a dull moment when he was around. He was later superseded as my No. 1 hero by one Brian 'George' Statham whom I greatly admired for his consistency and nagging accuracy.

MY IDEA OF THE PERFECT BOWLER
Fred Titmus as a slow bowler and Fred Trueman and Dennis Lillee as pacemen. They all had a simplicity of action and superb control. Each of them produced maximum effectiveness from minimum effort and all three were able to swing the ball away from the right-handed batsman. Trueman and Lillee did their work on a much more violent basis than Titmus but he was equally effective in his own quiet way, mastering the art of disguising his faster delivery and of making the away swinger drift off course just as the bamsman prepared for what he thought was going to be a full-face connection.

MY IDEA OF THE PERFECT BATSMAN
Garry Sobers who was blessed with all the ability and all the grace you could wish for. He could attack or defend or be purely Sobers in that he went his own sweet way with unorthodox strokes that left bowlers scratching their heads wondering how to contain him. He had a full repertoire of shots that meant he was equipped to deal with any situation. Had Barry Richards had the challenge of more Test cricket, I feel he might have reached the same heights and recognition as the genius Sobers.

John Snow was born in Peopleton, Worcestershire, on 13 October 1941. An aggressive and penetrating fast bowler, he took 202 wickets in 49 Tests at an average 26.66. His 31 wickets in the 1970–71 Test series in Australia laid the foundation for England's regaining of the Ashes for the first time in 12 years. The son of a vicar, he was a controversial character whose career was captured in the title of his autobiography: *Cricket Rebel*. His solid batting often proved invaluable to both Sussex and England. His highest Test score was an undefeated 59 against the West Indies at The Oval in 1966 when he and Ken Higgs shared a last-wicket stand of 128. He made a brief comeback with Warwickshire in one-day matches.

BRIAN STATHAM
Lancashire (1950–68)

MY CHILDHOOD BOWLING HERO
'Ted' McDonald, the Australian who played for Nelson in the Lancashire League and then qualified to represent Lancashire. He had one of the most graceful run-ups of any fast bowler and was so light and elegant on his way in to deliver the ball that he rarely left any foot marks even on the softest ground. I grew up surrounded by people talking about his achievements and in particular how his pace bowling had helped Lancashire win three County championships. When confronted by a class batsman – a Hobbs or a Bradman – they say he used to increase his speed to a lightning-fast pace yet losing nothing in his elegance. I would have loved to have watched him at his peak.

MY CHILDHOOD BATTING HERO

Sir Donald Bradman, fleet of foot and possessing an uncanny knack of finding gaps in the tightest field with a full range of shots. His career average of 95.14 and his Test average of 99.94 says it all. He was the greatest run maker the game has ever known and he could score big totals on any wicket and against the finest bowlers in the world of all speeds and varieties. He could drive, cut, hook, sweep – you name it and the shot was in his repertoire.

MY IDEA OF THE PERFECT BOWLER

It has surely got to be Sydney Barnes, who was a perfectionist capable of taking advantage of any ground conditions. There was no such thing as a 'good batting wicket' when he was operating with the ball. He had immaculate control of length, direction and swing, constantly making the batsmen play and demanding the best from his fielders. His 189 wickets in 27 Tests at an average 16.43 are figures that reveal just how deadly accurate he was against the top batsmen.

MY IDEA OF THE PERFECT BATSMAN

Bradman, of course, and Sir Frank Worrell. He was graceful, had good defensive technique, was a beautiful timer of the ball, possessed patience and was prepared to work hard. When necessary, he had the shots to take any attack apart. Both he and 'The Don' had the exceptional power of concentration that sets the great batsmen apart.

FOR THE RECORD

See page 42

DAVID STEELE
Northamptonshire and Derbyshire (1963–   )

MY CHILDHOOD BATTING HERO
Len Hutton, a batsman with a fine technique and full range of shots. He had tremendous discipline, concentration and dogged determination to go with his ability and while he was at the wicket you always had the feeling that England had a chance of victory.

MY CHILDHOOD BOWLING HERO
Fred Trueman was the bowler I most admired. He had pace, aggression and accuracy and would never concede that a batsman had got the better of him. His bowling was often hostile but he could also keep to a steady pace, concentrating on good line and length and waiting for the right moment to slip in his fastest delivery to the unsuspecting batsman.

MY IDEA OF THE PERFECT BATSMAN
Peter May, a great player for Surrey and England. He was a beautiful stylist who could make runs on both sides of the wicket with shots that were perfectly timed and placed. Especially strong on the on side, he was a magnificent exponent of the drive and you knew the ball was going to the boundary the moment it left his flashing bat.

MY IDEA OF THE PERFECT BOWLER
Bishen Bedi, India's masterly slow left-arm bowler. He had the most perfect action of any bowler and turned spin bowling into a great art. He had a bewildering variation of flight and spin and could deceive batsmen with subtle changes of pace. On top of all this he also had a great temperament and it was a memorable experience playing with him for Northants. I never tired of watching him in action.

FOR THE RECORD

David Steele was born at Stoke-on-Trent on 29 September 1941. He made a late entry on to the Test stage and in a short space of time established himself as one of the favourite cricketing heroes of the 1970s. He won the hearts of the public when, at the age of 33 but looking older because of prematurely grey hair, he made a stunning Test debut against Australia at Lord's in 1975. He shared a brave stand of 96 with Tony Greig, scoring 50 on his way to topping England's averages for that series with 365 runs at an average 60.83. He plays in spectacles and has a younger brother, John, who has been a regular with Leicestershire. A good-class left-arm spin bowler, he scored 1,000 runs in a season nine times for Northants before joining Derbyshire in 1979, briefly, as skipper.

BRIAN JOHNSTON'S
DREAM TEAM

 1 **LEN HUTTON**
 2 **BARRY RICHARDS**
 3 **VIV RICHARDS**
 4 **DON BRADMAN**
 5 **WALLY HAMMOND**
 6 **DENIS COMPTON**
 7 **GARRY SOBERS**
 8 **RICHIE BENAUD/JIM LAKER**
 9 **GODFREY EVANS**
10 **RAY LINDWALL**
11 **DENNIS LILLEE**
12th man: **KEITH MILLER**

'I have picked only from those on whom I have commentated in a Test match and have taken it that each player is

113

at the absolute peak of his form. The composition of the side was influenced by my desire for them to score a *minimum* of 450 runs off the first 100 overs. I am convinced they will need to bat only once and I defy anyone to bowl them out twice! Lindwall and Lillee will share the new ball, supported by Sobers in his fast role. The great Garfield will then share spin duties with either Laker or Benaud, depending where the match is played. If the venue is overseas, then Benaud will be my choice. In England, Laker will play – particularly if it's at Old Trafford! Hammond, Compton and Viv Richards will all be in reserve as support bowlers if needed. They are all marvellous in the field and I do not envisage a single catch being dropped. A dream team indeed.'

BRIAN JOHNSTON

BRIAN JOHNSTON, one of Britain's best-loved broadcasters, has for many years been an authoritative voice of cricket for the BBC radio team. One of his most memorable moments was being at the microphone in 1953 to describe the moment when Denis Compton swept the ball to the boundary at The Oval to regain the Ashes against Australia. His many radio shows have included *In Town Tonight* and *Down Your Way* but it's as the humorous and perceptive doyen of the cricket commentary box that he has his biggest following.

BOB TAYLOR
Derbyshire (1960–   )

MY CHILDHOOD BATTING HERO
Peter May was the batsman I most admired. He made it all seem so easy, stroking the ball almost effortlessly to the boundary with shots that were beautifully timed and

perfectly placed. Despite the responsibilities of captaincy he was still able to give complete concentration to his batting and he always looked in command of the situation regardless of the pressure placed on him.

MY CHILDHOOD BOWLING HERO
Jim Laker was the bowler who used to take my eye. His 19 wickets against Australia in the 1956 Test at Old Trafford made a big impression on a whole new generation of young cricket followers who, like me, were just starting to fall in love with the game.

MY CHILDHOOD WICKET-KEEPING HERO
Godfrey Evans, who was a bundle of energy behind the stumps for Kent and England. He was full of bounce and agility and few things got past him. His enthusiasm for the game spread to everybody around him and the action was never dull when he was keeping wicket.

MY IDEA OF THE PERFECT BATSMAN
Viv Richards, for his all-round batting technique on any wicket and in any conditions. He can be a ferocious hitter of the ball or can steer it to the boundary with the most delicate of touches.

MY IDEA OF THE PERFECT BOWLER
Dennis Lillee, who over the last decade has constantly produced 100 per cent effort and a deadly line and length. He is dangerous even when bowling at less than top speed because of the amount of movement he can get with the ball in the air or off the pitch. The nearest performance there has been to perfection from a bowler has to be the remarkable 1956 Test haul of 19 wickets by my boyhood hero Jim Laker.

MY IDEA OF THE PERFECT WICKET-KEEPER
Keith Andrew of Northants and England, who turned wicket-keeping into an art. He took over as the National Cricket Association's chief coach and is widely respected

for his deep knowledge of the game. Young cricketers could not be placed in better hands.

FOR THE RECORD

See page 52

FRED TITMUS
Middlesex and Surrey (1949–80)

MY CHILDHOOD BOWLING HERO
Jack Young, who was a fine left-arm orthodox spinner for Middlesex and England and whose career bridged the war. He could make the ball turn on the least helpful wickets and had total command of length and direction. Proof of his accuracy is that he managed to bowl 11 consecutive maidens against Don Bradman's magnificent 1948 Australian team in the Trent Bridge Test. He took 100 wickets in a season eight times and he had a pleasing personality that appealed to spectators and players alike.

MY CHILDHOOD BATTING HERO
It has to be Denis Compton. There will never be another like him for enterprise and entertainment. He was a dashing batsman who didn't know the meaning of the word retreat. Denis was the despair of coaches because he never played by the book but made it up as he went along. It was a joy to watch him when he was going for runs.

MY IDEA OF THE PERFECT BOWLER
Derek Shackleton, of Hampshire. He had a lovely action and could bowl all day. I never once saw him bowl a bad ball. Fred Trueman was another I greatly admired. He not

only *talks* a good game of cricket, he could play it as well and produced a whole string of outstanding performances for Yorkshire and England.

MY IDEA OF THE PERFECT BATSMAN
Greg Chappell, an Australian batsman with a classic English style. He has a wide range of textbook shots and is always looking to use them. There is a natural grace and ease about his game and he sets out to dominate the bowlers from the first ball he receives.

FOR THE RECORD

Fred Titmus was born at St Pancras, London, on 24 November 1932. He took 153 wickets and scored 1,449 runs for England in 53 Tests. At 16 he was the youngest player to make his debut for Middlesex with whom he played for more than a quarter of a century. He was briefly a Surrey player-coach at the back end of his career and set a unique record of playing first-class cricket in five decades. A boating accident in the West Indies in 1967–68 led to him having three toes amputated but he played on for another 12 years before retiring to run a post office in Hertfordshire. While mainly a spin-bowler, he was also an accomplished batsman and he completed the double of 100 wickets and 1,000 runs in a season eight times.

FRED TRUEMAN
Yorkshire and Derbyshire (1949–69)

MY CHILDHOOD BOWLING HERO
Harold Larwood was the bowler I used to hear so much about when I was a lad and he was my hero, though I never went to a county cricket ground. I used to read all about the great players in the newspapers that I delivered

every morning but it wasn't until I became a Yorkshire League player that I began to take a real interest in other players and Ray Lindwall took over as the bowler that I most admired.

MY CHILDHOOD BATTING HERO
Sir Leonard Hutton, and not just because he was a Yorkshireman. He is the greatest batsman I have ever seen and no one has come near his artistry. His bat looked as wide as a barn door to bowlers and he had the knack of being able to hit the ball early or late as the situation demanded. He was as light on his feet as a ballet dancer and could place his shots with pinpoint accuracy.

MY IDEA OF THE PERFECT BOWLER
Ray Lindwall, who was very fast yet had a medium-pace bowler's accuracy and the ability to move the ball either way. He had a beautifully controlled run-up and a nice, easy action. It has been said that if Tchaikovsky had seen Lindwall approaching the wicket, with the slow start and the graceful acceleration coming to the point of balance and delivery, he would have written a symphony to commemorate him.

MY IDEA OF THE PERFECT BATSMAN
It has to be Sir Leonard Hutton, who had the ability to score runs on all types of wickets and against the best bowling attacks. He was a true master.

FOR THE RECORD

See page 29

DEREK UNDERWOOD
Kent (1963–   )

MY CHILDHOOD BOWLING HERO
Fred Trueman. He was aggressive, determined, a good tactical bowler and, above all, very quick. All batsmen were his natural enemies and he was not happy until he had seen them off with bowling that could be hostile and also cunning. His away swinger was a gem of a delivery that time and again had batsmen reluctantly giving a snick to the slips.

MY CHILDHOOD BATTING HERO
Peter May and Colin Cowdrey shared top place in my affections. Both were pure artists who could play their strokes on all wickets and in any conditions. They could get the ball away to the boundary off their front or back foot and were able to drive past the bowler with clinical precision.

MY IDEA OF THE PERFECT BOWLER
Dennis Lillee is the bowler I have admired more than any other. He showed immense dedication to come back after a back injury that threatened his career. His pace, direction and competitive spirit make him a threat whatever the conditions. He has got guile to go with his speed, making the ball swerve or cut away and he can be as dangerous and intimidating with the old ball as with the new. His world record haul of Test wickets is all the proof that is needed of his great ability.

MY IDEA OF THE PERFECT BATSMAN
If I had to choose a batsman to play for my life I would pick between Ian Chappell, Geoff Boycott and Basil D'Oliveira. If I wanted to watch a batsman for sheer brilliance it would be between Viv Richards and Barry Richards but with a gun to my head I would finally select Garry Sobers as *the* king. Sobers had it all – style,

panache, authority and every stroke in the book and some of his own invention. If there is any such thing as perfection then Sobers was as close to it as can be.

FOR THE RECORD

See page 47

FRANK BRUNO'S
DREAM TEAM

1 **PERCY HOLMES** *(Larry)*
2 **CLYDE WALCOTT** *(Jersey Joe)*
3 **ABID ALI** *(Muhammad)*
4 **WARWICK ARMSTRONG** *(Henry)*
5 **RAY ROBINSON** *(Sugar Ray)*
6 **TONY LEWIS** *(Ted 'Kid')*
7 **KEITH MILLER** *(Freddie)*
8 **FREDDIE BROWN** *(Joe)*
9 **MAX WALKER** *(Mickey)*
10 **IAN JOHNSON** *(Jack)*
11 **CHARLIE GRIFFITH** *(Emil)*

'This is a knockout of a dream team! Every player has appeared in Test cricket and each of them shares a surname with a winner of a world boxing championship. I have to own up and admit I could not have selected the side without the help of my manager Terry Lawless, who loves cricket almost as much as he loves boxing. Terry's idea of heaven would be to watch Ian Botham facing Michael Holding at Lord's during the day and then going to Wembley in the evening to see Sugar Ray Robinson at his peak fighting Marvin Hagler. Clyde Walcott would be the wicket-keeper.'

FRANK BRUNO

FRANK BRUNO, Britain's great heavyweight boxing hope, is a Londoner born to West Indian parents and his cricket loyalties are torn between the West Indies and England. He has the power and physique that would have made him a fast bowler in the Wes Hall mould but he preferred throwing punches to cricket balls.

DILIP VENGSARKAR
Bombay (1975–)

MY CHILDHOOD BATTING HERO
Ajit Wadekar was the batsman who meant something very special to me. I never used to miss the opportunity of watching him bat in Bombay. From the moment he walked out to bat he had my rapt attention. There was a coolness and detachment about him that appealed to me and he always looked so in control of the situation.

MY CHILDHOOD BOWLING HERO
I was at school and totally devoted to cricket when Dennis Lillee was at his peak. I thought he was one of the greatest fast bowlers then and since playing against him I have had no reason to change that assessment.

MY IDEA OF THE PERFECT BATSMAN
Vivian Richards. He can be totally dominating at the wicket against any attack and on any surface. There is just

no stopping him when he has made up his mind to go for runs.

MY IDEA OF THE PERFECT BOWLER
I must select my hero Dennis Lillee. Apart from his great bowling pace and skill he also has tremendous willpower and determination. What a man to have on your side!

FOR THE RECORD

Dilip Vengsarkar was born in Bombay on 6 April 1956. He is a graceful right-handed batsman who occasionally opens for India but more usually comes in at number three. A buzz went round the cricket world that India had unveiled another outstanding batsman when he averaged 59.57 in six Tests against the West Indies in 1978–79, including an unbeaten 157 at Calcutta and 109 at Delhi. He confirmed his early promise the following summer during the tour of England when his 103 in the second innings of the Lord's Test was one of the highlights of the series. He bats with a maturity beyond his years and looks certain to be a prolific run maker for India for many seasons to come.

PETER WALKER
Glamorgan (1954–72)

MY CHILDHOOD BATTING HERO
I grew up in Johannesburg until I was 16 and so my boyhood heroes were South African cricketers. The batsman I most admired was Transvaal opener Bruce Mitchell who averaged 48.88 in 42 Tests. He was a classical player with a copybook defence and with the strokes to push the score along once he had laid the proper foundation for his team.

MY CHILDHOOD BOWLING HERO

My favourite bowler was the bespectacled 'Tufty' Mann, a slow left-arm specialist with Natal and Eastern Province. He had the sort of accuracy and control that could pin down the greatest batsmen. During 1947 he had the distinction of bowling eight successive maiden overs to Denis Compton and Bill Edrich. Nobody else could claim that during a summer when the 'terrible twins' ran riot.

MY IDEA OF THE PERFECT BATSMAN

There's no such thing but Garry Sobers comes closest. He is the only man I've ever played against who if he were to say, 'Today I'm going to get 100' would inspire me to go out and bet on it. I was at slip for Glamorgan the day he hit his record six successive sixes off Malcolm Nash. The last strike sent the ball sailing out of the ground towards Swansea Guildhall a mile away. That somehow summed up his standing in the game – way above everybody else.

MY IDEA OF THE PERFECT BOWLER

Don Shepherd, the Glamorgan off-spinner who was the best uncapped bowler of his generation. He had everything – great innate skill, stamina, perseverance, and, above all, heart. He was an excellent 'reader' of opposing batsmen and would be as committed and accurate at the end of the day as at the beginning.

FOR THE RECORD

Peter Walker was born in Bristol on 17 February 1936. He was a superb all-rounder who had a contribution to make in every phase of the game, whether with the bat, the ball or in the field. Standing 6ft 4in and with a telescopic reach, he was a magnificent short-leg fieldsman who took a record number of catches for Glamorgan including eight in a match against Derbyshire at Swansea in 1970. Selected by England for three Tests, he scored more than 1,000 runs in a season 11 times and performed the double in 1961 with 1,347 runs and 101 wickets. He is now an author and television broadcaster who has got interviewing down to a fine art, as he proved with his long series of teatime conversations with cricket personalities on BBC-2.

DOUG WALTERS
New South Wales (1962–81)

MY CHILDHOOD BATTING HERO
Sir Garfield Sobers, a true cricketing genius who could literally win matches off his own bat. I was at school when he first started to establish himself as one of the world's great players and later had the privilege of playing against him. Whether it was with the bat or the ball, he brought an aura and excitement to every game in which he played.

MY CHILDHOOD BOWLING HERO
Wesley Hall, a magnificent fast bowler who had a beautiful action and could make the ball kick and rear on perfectly good wickets.

MY IDEA OF THE PERFECT BATSMAN
Greg Chappell and Viv Richards rolled into one would produce *the* perfect batsman. Greg has excellent technique and times the ball beautifully, while Viv is one of the most imaginative and inventive batsmen of all time.

MY IDEA OF THE PERFECT BOWLER
Dennis Lillee, who for heart, stamina and pure bowling talent is out on his own. In his early days he was a fast, hostile bowler with a classical action but has since developed into a real craftsman who thinks before he delivers and traps batsmen with crafty changes of pace and direction.

FOR THE RECORD

Doug Walters was born at Dundog, New South Wales, on 21 December 1945. English cricket followers rarely saw the best of Walters who in Australia is rated one of the all-time great batsmen. He was an adventurous stroke-player who averaged 48.26 runs for Australia in 74 Tests. A procession of West Indian bowlers will vouch for the fact that he could, on his day, be as powerful as any batsman in the world. In four Tests against the West Indies in Australia in 1968–69 he made 699 runs including 242 and 103 in the Sydney Test. Four years later in the West Indies he averaged 71.00 runs in five Tests and in 1976–77 he scored a century between lunch and tea at Port of Spain. He was a useful medium-pace swing bowler and a brilliant fielder in the covers.

WASIM BARI
Pakistan International Airways and Pakistan (1966–)

MY CHILDHOOD HEROES
Godfrey Evans was the wicket-keeper I always admired because he had bags of enthusiasm to go with his great agility and safe hands. My favourite bowlers were Fazal Mahmood, Ray Lindwall and Alec Bedser, all of whom were deadly accurate and capable of producing match-winning bursts of brilliance. Rohan Kanhai and Sir Garfield Sobers were the batsmen whose performances I used to look for because both were dashing players who went for their shots regardless of the pressure or the conditions.

MY IDEA OF THE PERFECT WICKET-KEEPER
I would place Alan Knott and Bob Taylor equal. Both are model wicket-keepers from whom youngsters can learn by

watch.ng them when they are behind the stumps. They have perfect balance and their positioning is always exactly right.

MY IDEA OF THE PERFECT BATSMAN
Sir Garfield Sobers, for whom 'perfect cricketer' would be a more fitting title. He could score runs and take wickets on all types of wickets and could dominate a match from beginning to end.

FOR THE RECORD

Wasim Bari, was born in Pakistan on 23 March 1948. He was Pakistan's regular number one wicket-keeper for 14 years from 1967 and is also a competent right-handed batsman. His wicket-keeping is safe and reliable without being fussy. He set a world record against New Zealand in 1979 when he caught seven of the first eight batsmen in the first innings of the Auckland Test. Wasim also had a memorable match against England at Headingley in 1971 when he held eight catches and scored 63 valuable runs. He has a good tactical mind and has captained Pakistan.

BOB WILLIS
Surrey and Warwickshire (1969–   )

MY CHILDHOOD BOWLING HERO
Brian Statham, who was a wonderfully accurate, undemonstrative and totally dedicated bowler. He had marvellous partnerships for England with Frank Tyson and Fred Trueman and was always prepared to bowl himself into the ground for his captain and his team.

MY CHILDHOOD BATTING HERO

Garry Sobers. He was such a gifted and exciting player who could play unbelievable strokes in any conditions. Garry was a match winner with bat or ball and had a style and flair that made him the hero of any schoolboy lucky to see him in action.

MY IDEA OF THE PERFECT BOWLER

Dennis Lillee. He is effective in any conditions and in any situation and capable of turning a game with an inspired spell of bowling. He can even bowl fast leg-breaks on a dead slow pitch!

MY IDEA OF THE PERFECT BATSMAN

Peter May. He was quietly destructive but still pleasing to the eye with strokes that were always played with control and composure. There was an almost regal air about him at the wicket where he was totally commanding and looking to dominate the bowlers.

FOR THE RECORD

Bob Willis was born in Sunderland on 30 May 1949. He is a born fighter who delights in proving critics wrong and emerged as an inspiring captain of England after twice being written off as finished following a succession of injuries. A 6ft 6in long-limbed giant, he started his first-class career with Surrey, making his debut in 1969. He flew out to Australia in 1970–71 as a replacement for injured Alan Ward and quickly established himself as a key man in the England squad. The following year he joined Warwickshire where, despite being plagued by injuries, he proved himself one of England's few world-class pace bowlers. He motivated team-mates by example and refuses to concede defeat until the final ball had been bowled. His retirement from first-class cricket in 1984 leaves the game poorer and the England attack for less effective.

JIMMY GREAVES'S
DREAM TEAM

1 **ARTHUR MILTON** *(Arsenal)*
2 **BILL EDRICH** *(Spurs)*
3 **WILLIE WATSON** *(Huddersfield/Sunderland)*
4 **DENIS COMPTON** *(Arsenal)*
5 **PATSY HENDREN** *(Manchester City)*
6 **IAN BOTHAM** *(Scunthorpe United)*
7 **BRIAN CLOSE** *(Bradford City)*
8 **LESLIE COMPTON** *(Arsenal)*
9 **GRAHAM CROSS** *(Leicester City)*
10 **JIM CUMBES** *(West Brom)*
11 **JIM STANDEN** *(West Ham)*
12th man: **CHRIS BALDERSTONE** *(Huddersfield)*

'I have gone for a team of footballing cricketers, all of whom have played football at League level. Whether playing with the big ball or the small red one, this would prove a formidable team. If dreams came true, I would have been a double international at football and cricket. My boyhood ambition was to follow Godfrey Evans behind the stumps for England but by the time I got into football the days of being an all-rounder – soccer in the winter and cricket in the summer – were drawing to an end. I have never lost my love for cricket and play and watch it whenever I can. As for all boys growing up in the 1940s and 1950s, Denis Compton was a hero of mine. His sporting life, goals for Arsenal and runs for Middlesex and England must have been just about perfect.'

JIMMY GREAVES

JIMMY GREAVES, one of the greatest goal scorers in football history and now a popular television personality and successful author, was a near-County class wicket-keeper who might have made the grade with Essex but for being ordered by his first club,

Chelsea, to give all his concentration to football. Cricket's loss was football's gain. He scored a record 357 First Division goals for Chelsea, Tottenham and West Ham and netted 44 goals in 57 England appearances.

BOB WOOLMER
Kent (1968–)

MY CHILDHOOD BATTING HERO
Colin Cowdrey and Ted Dexter were the two batsmen who brightened my schooldays with their stylish batting. Dexter had a cavalier approach to the game and there were always fireworks when he was at the wicket. Cowdrey was a gifted artist who served the game with distinction and it was a pleasure to play with him when I joined Kent.

MY CHILDHOOD BOWLING HERO
Brian Statham and Freddie Trueman claimed my admiration with their attacking partnership for England. They were the ideal balance for each other – Trueman genuinely quick and hostile, Statham accurate and totally committed. England have had few better new ball partners.

MY IDEA OF THE PERFECT BATSMAN
A combination of Barry and Viv Richards would be complete perfection. Both are exciting stroke players who like to get on with making their shots from the moment they arrive at the wicket. If you could combine their strengths you would have an unbeatable batsman.

MY IDEA OF THE PERFECT BOWLER
If you could mix the control and speed of Dennis Lillee

with the height and guile of Joel Garner I reckon you would have a supreme bowler. A Lillee-Garner combination bowling against a mix of Viv Richards and Barry Richards would be quite a confrontation!

FOR THE RECORD

Bob Woolmer was born in Kanpur, India, on 15 May 1948. He is a talented all-rounder who has made 19 Test appearances for England and has scored three centuries – all against Australia. A useful medium-fast bowler, his best returns have been seven for 47 against Sussex in 1979 and six for nine in a John Player League match against Derby at Chesterfield in 1979 and he performed a hat-trick for MCC against the Australians at Lord's in 1975. He scored a century before lunch against Derby, again at Chesterfield in 1979. In 1975 he scored the slowest of all England centuries against Australia, taking six hours 35 minutes. A back injury as forced his premature retirement and in the winter of 1985 he moved to South Aftica for a new career as a coach and administrator.

SECTION THREE
FINEST OF THE FINEST

Seventy-five Test stars recall their most memorable performances

DENNIS AMISS *(Warwickshire and England)*: I scored an unbeaten 262 for England against the West Indies in the second Test at Sabina Park, Jamaica, in 1974. I was at the wicket for 570 minutes and we managed to salvage a draw. We had already lost the first Test and while I was at the wicket the thought kept going through my mind that I had to hang on to keep our hopes alive for the rest of the series. This knock gave me a Test aggregate of 1,356 runs within a period of 12 months.

GEOFF ARNOLD *(Surrey, Sussex and England)*: The performance I recall above all others is taking six for 46 for England against India in New Delhi on the 1972–73 tour. What made it particularly memorable was that no other pace bowler had succeeded in getting wickets on a ground that was infamous as a graveyard for bowlers. The wicket was like a strip of rolled mud but the ball made impressions as I dug it in and this enabled it to seam. We won the match shortly after lunch on Christmas Day when skipper Tony Lewis and Tony Greig shared an unbroken fifth wicket stand of 101. It was England's first ever victory in Delhi and the first win in India for 21 years.

TREVOR BAILEY *(Essex and England)*: The 1953 Test series against Australia stands out in my memory because it ended with the Ashes being returned to England after a close and absorbing series. I particularly recall the second Test at Lord's when on the final day Willie Watson and I shared a 163-run fifth-wicket partnership which lasted from 12.42 p.m. until 40 minutes before the close. Willie scored 109 in 346 minutes and I managed 71 in 257 minutes. It was a necessary rearguard action which helped to pull England back from what at one time looked certain defeat.

ALEC BEDSER *(Surrey and England)*: I took seven wickets for 55 in the first innings of the first Test against Australia at Trent Bridge in 1953. This gave me a lot of satisfaction but I was even happier with my performance in the second innings when I took seven for 44. I finished the series with 39 wickets and the best thing of all about it was that we regained the Ashes.

IAN BOTHAM *(Somerset and England)*: Obviously the 1981 Headingley Test is a happy recent memory but I dig back to 1974 for my most memorable performance outside the Test arena. I was in my first full season with Somerset and skipper Brian Close selected me at the last minute for the vital Benson and Hedges quarter-final against Hampshire at Taunton. We were struggling at 113 for seven in reply to Hampshire's 182 when I came to the wicket. I had not even faced a ball when we lost another wicket without a run being added. Defeat looked inevitable. We needed 70 runs off the next 15 overs and only two wickets were left. I decided it was worth having a hit-or-miss bash and started to find the boundary. Hampshire called the great Andy Roberts back to their attack to try to regain the initiative. He produced a bouncer that almost did the trick. The ball smashed me in the mouth and I dropped like a KO'd boxer. A couple of my teeth were broken and I was spitting blood. They brought me a glass of water from the pavilion and asked if I wanted to go off. But I shook off my dizziness and insisted on batting on. I continued where I had left off, throwing the bat at everything and I managed to get Roberts away to the boundary for the winning run off the last ball before the final over. I was 45 not out and minus a couple of teeth. The pleasure I got out of that performance was worth all the pain.

GEOFF BOYCOTT *(Yorkshire and England)*: It was at Headingley, Leeds, in August 1977 when I completed my century of centuries while playing for England against Australia in the fourth Test. Purely by chance we were playing on my home ground when I became the first batsman to score a hundredth first-class century in a Test match. What made it all the more memorable was the warmth of the reception I was given by the public. It was all very emotional and the memory will last with me for ever. I went on to score 191 and we won by an innings and 85 runs to regain the Ashes.

MIKE BREARLEY *(Middlesex and England)*: I was playing for MCC Under-25s against North Zone at Peshawar in 1967 and after reaching my century decided to have a slog. Suddenly I found myself on 160 and steadied myself, deciding to go for a double century. Once I was past 200 I started slogging even harder and rumour had it that the scorers fled up the Khyber Pass! It was also said that as I approached my triple hundred, Hanif Mohammad telephoned because he was worried that I would try to beat his world record score of 499! Seriously though, I went on to an unbeaten 312 which remained the highest score of my career. In all fairness, I should point out that the North Zone fielding left something to be desired.

DAVID BROWN *(Warwickshire and England)*: England were playing Australia in the third Test in Sydney on the 1965–66 tour. Skipper Mike Smith tossed the second new ball to me during their first innings. In my first over I took three vital wickets which helped set up a memorable victory by an innings and 93 runs. The foundation for England's first win over Australia in 11 matches was laid by Geoff Boycott and Bob Barber who shared a superb opening partnership of 234 in 240 minutes.

TOM CARTWRIGHT *(Warwickshire, Somerset, Glamorgan and England)*: Scoring 210 runs for Warwickshire against Middlesex at Nuneaton in 1962. It was the highest score of my career and came during a memorable season when I completed the double of 100 wickets and 1,000 runs. I also had my best bowling figures that season – eight for 39 for Warwickshire against Somerset at Weston-super-Mare.

BRIAN CLOSE *(Yorkshire, Somerset and England)*: I have to select the Test innings at Lord's in 1963 when I managed to defy the West Indian pace bowlers Wes Hall and Charlie Griffith. They had been causing us a few problems and I decided to take the initiative by moving down the wicket to them. My policy brought me a few bruises but, more important, I got 70 runs in our second innings. There was a dramatic finish to the match with Colin Cowdrey at the wicket with the last man David Allen despite having a fractured left arm in plaster. We needed six runs off the last ball to win and the game finished as a draw after a nail-biting climax.

DENIS COMPTON *(Middlesex and England)*: It was for England against Australia at Old Trafford in 1948. I edged a ball from Ray Lindwall into my face and had to leave the field to have six stitches inserted in a gash on my brow. I had scored just four runs and England were in trouble at 32 for two. I resumed my innings at 119 for five and managed to make an unbeaten 145.

COLIN COWDREY *(Kent and England)*: It was in the third Test against Australia in Melbourne in 1955. Len Hutton, Bill Edrich, Peter May and Denis Compton had fallen to Keith Miller and Ray Lindwall for 20. I managed to score 102 in our total of 191. This was my first Test century and, thanks largely to Frank Tyson's devastating bowling, we went on to win the match and the series.

MIKE DENNESS *(Kent, Essex and England)*: I am happiest to remember my 188 for England against Australia at Melbourne in the sixth and final Test of the 1974–75 tour. We had been given a torrid time by pace partners Lillee and Thomson and I had dropped myself for the fourth Test. I managed to win back some self-respect in Melbourne, Keith Fletcher had a superb knock of 146 and my innings was the highest score by an England captain during a Test in Australia. We won by an innings and I was tremendously proud of the character and fighting qualities shown by the entire team.

TED DEXTER *(Sussex and England)*: Scoring my second Test hundred for England against West Indies in Barbados in 1960 is the performance I remember best of all from my career. What made it most satisfying was that it was my first century against bowling of real quality which had already tested some of the established stars. I got an unbeaten 136. Ken Barrington was also among the runs in that innings with 128. England won by 256 runs with 110 minutes to spare on the final day. We had set West Indies a target of 501 runs in ten hours and had them all out for 244. Rohan Kanhai was the only West Indian batsman to really threaten us and I had the good fortune to get his wicket thanks to a catch by Mike Smith after Kanhai had made 110. It was a dramatic match to say the least, with a crowd riot forcing a premature end to play on the third day after a controversial run-out incident.

BILL EDRICH *(Middlesex and England)*: I scored 219 in the 'Timeless' Test against South Africa in the final Test in Durban in 1938–39. It was supposed to be played to a finish but after ten days play and a record aggregate of 1,981 runs the teams had to concede a draw because we were booked on a voyage for home. At the close, England were 654 for five. There is a permanent reminder of my feat because in those days anybody scoring a Test century in Durban had a tree planted in their honour. So an Edrich tree grows in Durban!

JOHN EDRICH *(Surrey and England)*: I scored 310 not out for England against New Zealand at Headingley in 1965. It was another of my 'comebacks' into the England side and for the first 35 minutes I scratched around without scoring. Then everything I tried to do came off and I started to score runs all over the place during a day and three quarters at the wicket. I shared a partnership of 369 in 339 minutes with Ken Barrington and my five sixes and 52 fours created a new Test record for boundaries in one innings. England won the match by an innings and 187 runs.

GODFREY EVANS *(Kent and England)*: So many wonderful memories come flooding back and I find it difficult to be pinned down to a single answer. There was my 'nought' in 95 minutes in partnership with Denis Compton to save the fourth Test against Australia in Adelaide in 1946–47. Then there was the other extreme – 98 before lunch against India at Lord's in 1952. My outstanding memory of keeping wicket takes me back to the first morning of the fifth Test against Australia at Melbourne in 1950–51. I have never known the ball move around so much, particularly when big Alec Bedser was bowling. He took ten wickets in the match and we beat the Aussies for the first time since 1938.

KEITH FLETCHER *(Essex and England)*: Geoff Arnold and I shared an unbroken last-wicket stand of 92 in 87 minutes to save England from defeat against New Zealand at Lord's in 1973. I hit two sixes and 21 fours in my total of 178 not out and we salvaged a draw after New Zealand had a massive total of 551 in their first innings.

MIKE GATTING *(Middlesex and England)*: It was in a dramatic and eventful match for Middlesex against Lancashire at Lord's in 1978. We were chasing 130 to win in our second innings and Colin Croft was spearheading the Lancashire attack on a helpful wicket. Ian Gould got a nasty blow on the head during a bumper barrage from Croft and was taken to hospital for treatment. I managed to score 88 but was out with 13 runs still required and just two wickets left. Mike Selvey and John Emburey, who was at the wicket for an hour before he scored a run, helped us through to a thrilling one-wicket victory.

SUNIL GAVASKAR *(Bombay, Somerset and India)*: Every century I have scored has, of course, given me great satisfaction but it is a score of 57 that I remember with the greatest pleasure. I made the runs for India against England in the first innings of the second Test at Old Trafford in 1971. It was my first experience of facing genuine speed on a green top and I was delighted to get my half century in conditions that I had never before experienced. John Price and John Lever shared the new ball and I managed to keep them out until giving Alan Knott a catch behind off a good ball from Price.

GRAHAM GOOCH *(Essex and England)*: My 120 for Essex against Surrey in the 1979 Benson & Hedges Cup Final at Lord's sticks in my mind as the most satisfying innings I have ever played. The main reason it meant so much to me is that it helped Essex win their first-ever trophy. That whole day at Lord's remains the best day I have ever had in cricket. It was nice to win something after such a long time and it set us up for greater successes.

DAVID GOWER *(Leicestershire and England)*: My most gratifying innings was my 154 not out for England against the West Indies at Sabina Park, Jamaica, on the 1981 tour. The score was ten for two when I came in with the best part of two days to play for England to save the game. Peter Willey and I put on 136 for the fourth wicket and then after Ian Botham and Roland Butcher had been dismissed Paul Downton joined me and gave a stubborn performance, particularly against some hostile bowling by Michael Holding. At the close I was unbeaten after seven and three quarter hours at the wicket. Paul and I were together with the score at 302 for six and the match was drawn.

TOM GRAVENEY *(Gloucestershire, Worcestershire and England)*: The personal performance I rate above all others was for England against the West Indies in the second Test at Lord's in 1966. I was making my comeback to the Test stage after three years and it was my 39th birthday. The crowd were marvellous and gave me a tremendous ovation, applauding me all the way to the wicket before I'd faced a ball. It was a wonderful yet frightening experience because I did not want to let them down after such a spontaneous show of warmth. I managed to produce my best form in the evening session against a West Indies attack that included Wes Hall, Charlie Griffith, Garry Sobers and Lance Gibbs. My form deserted me the next morning but I rate the 96 I scored as one of my better knocks, particularly as at the time Hall and Griffith were presenting problems to so many batsmen.

KIM HUGHES *(Western Australia and Australia)*: The innings that will always remain prominent in my memory is my 100 not out against West Indies on the first day of the first Test of the 1981–82 series at Melbourne. Above all I will recall the support of the MCG crowd. They really got behind me and helped me through the crisis after I had gone to the wicket with our score at four for 20 and with Holding, Roberts, Garner and Croft in full cry. I had reached 77 when our ninth wicket fell and Terry Alderman came in. He gave me magnificent support, shoring up one end while I went for my shots. I reached my 100 with a satisfying square cut off Garner. It was my eleventh four and I was at the wicket for 262 minutes. Terry was out to Croft soon after but we had laid the foundation for a victory by 58 runs.

SIR LEN HUTTON *(Yorkshire and England)*: I remember my then world record, 364 against Australia in 1938, for the strain and my 145 against the Aussies at Lord's in 1953 for the satisfaction. The 364 innings was an exhausting marathon that lasted 13 hours 20 minutes. It seemed like a lifetime and I was completely drained at the end of it after concentrating non-stop. At the other extreme, the knock in 1953 was one of those that just flowed. I really enjoyed it because it was at Lord's, a ground where I always felt a little over-awed because of the great traditions of the place. I had the added responsibility of being skipper and so was doubly determined to give the innings the best possible start. We finally drew the match thanks to a classic rearguard action by Trevor Bailey and Willie Watson who were together most of the final day in a fifth-wicket partnership that put on 163 invaluable runs. Our morale was extremely high at the end of the match and we went on to regain the Ashes.

RAY ILLINGWORTH *(Yorkshire, Leicestershire and England)*: The performance I remember above all others was in a County match for Yorkshire against Kent at the picturesque ground at Dover in 1964. I took 14 wickets for 101 and to make it even more memorable I also scored a century.

IMRAN KHAN *(Lahore, Oxford University, Worcestershire, Sussex and Pakistan)*: I was playing for Sussex against Derbyshire at Eastbourne at the back end of the 1981 season and we needed to win to keep in contention with Notts for the championship. The match on the last day was heading for a draw, with Derby refusing to declare and set us a target. On a dead wicket I got four wickets in five balls and then scored a hundred in quick time to clinch victory in the last over.

DOUG INSOLE *(Essex and England)*: My most memorable performance came in a match for Essex against Surrey at Clacton in 1956 when Surrey were at the peak of their phenomenal successes of the 1950s. They had Alec Bedser, Peter Loader, Jim Laker and Tony Lock together in a great attacking force. Needing 253 to win in our second innings, we were quickly in trouble at 23 for three. I was at the wicket for two and a half hours during which I scored 115 to help Essex to victory by two wickets, to the undisguised delight of our biggest ever third-day crowd. To beat that magnificent Surrey team was pleasure enough but to have done it with a young side and by scoring runs against the clock enhanced that pleasure.

SYED KIRMANI *(Mysore and India)*: Two performances share an equal place of pleasure in my memory. Equalling the world record of six victims in a Test innings against New Zealand at Christchurch in 1976 gave me cause for celebration. I held three catches off the bowling of Mohinder Amarnath, three off the bowling of Madan Lal and I stumped Bev Congdon after a beautifully flighted ball from Bishen Bedi. The other outstanding memory is of an unbeaten innings of 101 for India against Australia at Bombay in 1979–80. I went in as night-watchman and scored my maiden Test century in five hours. We won the match by an innings and 100 runs.

ALAN KNOTT *(Kent and England)*: It was the last day of the final Test between West Indies and England at Georgetown in 1968 and we were battling to salvage a draw that would give us a one-nil victory in the series. I shared a four-hour stand with skipper Colin Cowdrey. At the end of play we were nine wickets down and I was lucky enough to be 73 not out. It was the second top score in the innings behind Colin who gave a real captain's performance in scoring 82.

JIM LAKER *(Surrey, Essex and England)*: It has to be my 19 wickets for 90 runs for England against Australia at Old Trafford in 1956. I suppose the most remarkable thing about it was that my Surrey 'twin' Tony Lock, almost unplayable on his day, could pick up only one wicket. The best ball I bowled in the match was the one that knocked over the great Neil Harvey's wicket in the first innings. I tried too hard to repeat it in the second innings and sent down a loose full toss. Neil tried to give it the heave-ho treatment it deserved but succeeded only in hitting it

140

down Colin Cowdrey's throat for a rare pair. Poor Neil chucked his bat up in the air in disgust. It was one of those matches when just everything went right for me.

DAVID LARTER *(Northamptonshire and England)*: I remember hitting a purple patch while bowling for Northants against Leicestershire in a Gillette Cup match at Grace Road in 1964. I broke through the Leicester batting with a five-wicket spell for 24 runs and we shot them out for just 56 runs in 26.2 overs. Mike Kettle did the damage from the other end with four wickets for 19 runs. We were the first team to win in the competition by ten wickets. I had many better figures but this was my most satisfying spell of bowling.

JOHN LEVER *(Essex and England)*: I'll never forget my Test debut for England against India in Delhi in 1976. Quite a lot of pressure was taken off me when we batted first and, thanks to a glorious 179 by Dennis Amiss, 75 by Alan Knott and 53 from me, we totalled a solid 381. This cured my nerves and I managed to do well with the ball, taking seven for 46. 'Deadly' Derek Underwood claimed four wickets in their second innings and I took my match haul to ten for 70 as we clinched England's first ever victory by an innings in India.

TONY LEWIS *(Glamorgan and England)*: The innings that gave me the greatest pleasure was scoring 70 not out in an unbeaten stand with Tony Greig to steer England to victory over India on Christmas Day in the first Test in New Delhi in 1972. It was my Test debut and, as captain, I felt extra responsibility as I walked to the wicket in the first innings. I made an inauspicious start with a duck, going leg before to that magician of spin Chandrasekhar. But, thank goodness, I made up for it in the second innings. Tony Greig and I shared a fifth-wicket partnership of 101 and were still together just after lunch for the winning run. It was England's first victory in Delhi and their first victory in India since 1951–52. India were fresh from just having beaten the West Indies and England in away Test series, so our victory tasted very sweet and made that a really memorable and happy Christmas.

DENNIS LILLEE *(Western Australia and Australia)*: The match I will always recall with fond memories is the Centenary Test between Australia and England in Melbourne in 1977. It was a pretty eventful game for me. I managed to take 11 wickets – six for 26 in the first innings and five for 139 in the second. But above what I achieved personally I will remember the great atmosphere in the ground and the feeling of nostalgia and camaraderie generated by all the great old Test players who had gathered for the match. It was a marvellous occasion, made even better by the fact that Australia won!

DAVID LLOYD *(Lancashire and England)*: Lancashire were struggling at 33 for three in reply to Gloucestershire's 266 in a Gillette Cup match at Old Trafford in 1978. Then Clive Lloyd and I came together to share a record 234 runs in an unbroken fourth-wicket stand. I was 121 not out and Clive 119 not out. We won by seven wickets and I got the Man of the Match award.

BRIAN LUCKHURST *(Kent and England)*: The innings that stands out in my memory was in a County match for Kent against Surrey at Blackheath in 1966. The wicket was in an appalling state, full of holes and with the ball going off at all unpredictable heights and angles. Somehow I managed to score 183 runs.

RODNEY MARSH *(Western Australia and Australia)*: The Centenary Test against England at Melbourne in 1977 is a match I'll never forget. I held five catches to break Wally Grout's Australian Test wicket-keeping record and I scored an unbeaten 110 in our second innings. What made it even more memorable was keeping wicket to Dennis Lillee's bowling. He produced the best performance I've ever seen and I was delighted to take four catches off his bowling to help him capture 11 wickets.

PETER MAY *(Surrey and England)*: The innings I remember above all others came in the first Test against the West Indies at Edgbaston in 1957. I scored 285 not out and shared a record fourth-wicket partnership of 411 with Colin Cowdrey. It was particularly satisfying for me as captain because at one stage we looked like suffering a heavy defeat. Sonny Ramadhin sent down 129 overs and a record 774 balls during the match, which finished drawn.

COLIN MILBURN *(Northamptonshire and England)*: I opened the innings for Western Australia against Queensland at Brisbane in 1968–69 and scored 62 before lunch. Then between lunch and tea I got a move on and added another 181 runs in two hours to take my score to 243, a record for Western Australia. I was out on my feet by the time the tea interval came. The temperature was round about 100 degrees and it was like an oven out in the middle. The tea break did nothing to revive me and I was so absolutely exhausted that I was out first ball in the last session!

ARTHUR MILTON *(Gloucestershire and England)*: I was playing for Gloucestershire against Notts on a badly crumbled wicket at Bristol in 1954. Notts included that fine Australian leg spinner Bruce Dooland in their attack and he was giving everybody trouble but I managed to score 111 runs and we went on to win by an innings and 45 runs.

ARTHUR McINTYRE *(Surrey and England)*: Though I have many happy recollections of keeping wicket it is a performance with the bat that provides my most satisfying memory. I scored my maiden first-class century for Surrey against Kent at The Oval in 1946 while sharing a 200 partnership with Geoff Whittaker. There was a capacity crowd, it was a beautiful day and the wicket was just right. Everything about it was perfect.

JOHN MURRAY *(Middlesex and England)*: England were in deep trouble against the West Indies at The Oval in 1966 when I joined Tom Graveney at the wicket with 166 for seven on the board. Tom and I put on 217 in 235 minutes. He scored a graceful 165 and I scored my one and only Test century, which was particularly pleasing for me as a wicket-keeper. Ken Higgs and John Snow shared a last-wicket stand of 128 and we finally totalled 527 and went on to win the match by an innings.

ALAN OAKMAN *(Sussex and England)*: It is an undefeated innings of 137 for Sussex against Lancashire at Hove in 1954 that gives me my happiest memory. I take the liberty of quoting the 1956 *Wisden* so that nobody can accuse me of getting carried away: 'Oakman played the varied, hostile Lancashire attack with supreme confidence for five hours and twenty minutes and hit 12 fours. This attack curtailed Statham, Hilton, Tattersall and Greenhoff, all England bowlers . . .'

JIM PARKS *(Sussex, Somerset and England)*: I was coaching in Trinidad when I was summoned to join the 1959–60 MCC tour of the West Indies as a replacement. I returned to Trinidad for the last Test and Mike Smith and I shared a record seventh-wicket stand of 197 to save the match. I scored 101 not out. To add to my memories of the match, I stumped the great Clyde Walcott off David Allen's bowling in the first innings and then caught him in the second innings off the bowling of the lovely Ken Barrington.

PAT POCOCK *(Surrey and England)*: Playing for England against the West Indies in an emotion-charged match in Trinidad in 1974, I took five wickets for 110 in the first innings. I bowled 43 overs and became only the third

Englishman to take five wickets in a Test innings on the Trinidad ground.

JOHN PRICE *(Middlesex and England)*: I think one's first Test is always going to be top of the memory list. My debut was against India in Bombay in 1964 and I happened to pick up five wickets, the first with a long hop and the second with a full toss! We played with ten men for most of the match because Mickey Stewart had one of those notorious tummy upsets and as four other players were also down with the complaint we had two wicket-keepers playing and only two specialist batsmen. I managed to score 32 in my only knock and we were delighted to get a draw considering all our handicaps. It was an eventful introduction to Test cricket.

PETER RICHARDSON *(Worcestershire, Kent and England)*: My maiden Test century for England against Australia at Old Trafford in 1956 is my No 1 memory. I shared century partnerships with Colin Cowdrey and David Sheppard. I'm told that Jim Laker did quite well in that match, too! This was the Test in which Jim took his world record 19 wickets, so my ton was slightly overshadowed.

BRIAN ROSE *(Somerset and England)*: I scored 110 not out for Somerset against the Australians at Bath in 1977. It is not the innings I remember as much as Somerset's victory by seven wickets, the first and only time that we had beaten the Aussies in 22 fixtures going back to 1893.

DEREK SHACKLETON *(Hampshire and England)*: I have memories of two performances that come quickly to mind. The first was for Hampshire against Somerset at Weston-super-Mare in 1955. I took 14 for 29 in the match including eight for four in the first innings. Five years later, playing for Hampshire against Warwickshire at Portsmouth, I took nine wickets for 30 runs in 19.3 overs.

PHIL SHARPE *(Yorkshire and England)*: Geoff Boycott scored 106 and I hit 83 as we chased runs in the second innings of the Lord's Test against the West Indies in 1969. For a time it looked as if we had lifted England into a winning position but then there were a couple of quick wickets after Geoff and I had been separated and the game finished in a draw.

REG SIMPSON *(Nottinghamshire and England)*: I completed my only century against Australia on my 31st birthday in the Melbourne Test of 1951. My final score in the first innings was 156 not out, including a last-wicket stand of 74 with Roy Tattersall who scored ten. We won the match by eight wickets, our first win against Australia since 1938.

ALAN SMITH *(Warwickshire and England)*: My most memorable performance was for England against Australia in the fourth Test at Adelaide in 1963. It was the best that I ever kept wicket. The bowlers were Freddie Trueman, Brian Statham, Ted Dexter, Ray Illingworth and Fred Titmus and I managed to hold on to five catches and allowed ten byes.

MIKE SMITH *(Leicestershire, Warwickshire and England)*: The innings I recall with the greatest satisfaction was for Warwickshire against Gloucestershire at Stroud in 1959. Gloucester batted first and scored 257. We just managed to avoid the follow-on with 115. We then bowled them out for 175 and clinched a thrilling victory by scoring 318 for six in our second innings. My contribution was an unbeaten 182.

JOHN SNOW *(Sussex, Warwickshire and England)*: The entire 1970–71 Test series remains in my memory as the highlight of my career. In particular there was my seven for 40 in the Sydney Test which helped us win by an innings and 299 runs. For me, the winning of the Ashes in Australia was the realisation of a dream.

BRIAN STATHAM *(Lancashire and England)*: I bowled throughout South Africa's second innings without a break in the Lord's Test of 1955 and my figures at the end were: 29 overs, 12 maidens, 7 wickets, 39 runs. The analysis would have been even better but for a couple of blatant catches being given not out by the umpire! The ball moved about a lot off the seam and we rushed South Africa out for 111 to win the match by 71 runs.

DICK SPOONER *(Warwickshire and England)*: My memory goes back to the Warwickshire match against Middlesex at Lord's in 1951. I was on the field with either batting or wicket-keeping pads on for all but about 30 minutes of the three days' play. What made it so satisfying was that I scored 96 runs in the first innings and 158 in the second.

DAVID STEELE *(Northants, Derbyshire and England)*: The first is always the best and I'll never forget my maiden century for England against the West Indies at Trent Bridge in 1976. I batted throughout the day and finally made 106. Viv Richards chose that Test to score a magnificent 232 and the match finished in a draw.

ROY TATTERSALL *(Lancashire and England)*: I'll always remember taking 12 wickets for 101 runs for England against South Africa in the 1951 Lord's Test. I took nine of the 14 wickets that fell on a rain-affected second day and we went on to clinch victory by ten wickets soon after lunch on the third day. The foundation for our win was laid by Denis Compton and Willie Watson, both of whom scored 79 runs in our first innings.

BOB TAYLOR *(Derbyshire and England)*: My most memorable match behind the stumps was when I set a world record of seven dismissals in an innings and ten in a match against India in the 1980 Golden Jubilee Test in Bombay. With the bat, I recall equalling my highest score of 97 against Australia in the second innings of the fifth Test in Adelaide on the 1978–79 tour. We looked as if we would lose until Geoff Miller and I put on 135 to set up a victory.

FRED TITMUS *(Middlesex, Surrey and England)*: The performance I will always remember was when I took seven for 79 in the first innings against Australia in the third Test at Sydney in 1962–63. I included 14 maidens in my 37 overs. On the second day I took four wickets for five runs in 58 balls. Unfortunately we lost the match by eight wickets. I managed to bowl Bobby Simpson but not before he had laid the foundation for an Australian victory with 91 runs, the highest score in the match.

ROGER TOLCHARD *(Leicestershire and England)*: I have two memories that stand out and both were performances with the bat rather than behind the wicket – getting 50 in my first Test for England against India in Calcutta in 1976–77 on a turning wicket and in front of 80,000 spectators . . . hitting Alan Ward for three sixes in four balls during a John Player League game against Derbyshire at Chesterfield.

FRED TRUEMAN *(Yorkshire, Derbyshire and England)*: Sorry, but I just cannot be pinned down to one memory. Every time I pulled on a Yorkshire or England sweater I felt an indescribable sense of pride. My 300th Test wicket provided me with a lot of pleasure, of course. It came against Australia at The Oval in 1964. I knocked back Ian Redpath's middle stump and had Graham McKenzie caught at slip off the last two balls before lunch. So, with 299 wickets in the bag, I was on a hat-trick. Neil Hawke, an old pal, faced me for my first ball after lunch and said before I bowled, 'Well, F. S. I wouldn't mind being the 300th, I suppose.' I tried really hard to complete the hat-trick but the ball went just wide of Neil's off-stump. I had to wait until my first delivery with the new ball. I whipped down an out-swinger, my favourite ball, and Neil edged it into the safe hands of Colin Cowdrey at slip. Neil, like a true sportsman, was first to congratulate me and to mark the event I gave him a bottle of champagne which remained unopened on his sideboard years later.

DEREK UNDERWOOD *(Kent and England)*: A thunderstorm appeared to have robbed England of victory against Australia at The Oval in 1968. But the spectators helped mop up the puddles and on a non-turning wicket I finished with seven for 50 to help England win the match with just three minutes to spare. Australian opener John Inverarity had defied us throughout the innings and was the last man out when I trapped him LBW. Five wickets fell in that dramatic last hour of play.

DILIP VENGSARKAR *(Bombay and India)*: I have wonderful memories of playing for India against England at Lord's. In 1979, I scored 103 in the second innings and shared 210 for the third wicket with Viswanath to help save the match. In the 1982 Lord's Test, I made 157 after England had forced us to follow on. I had the satisfaction of scoring my runs against a magnificent England seam attack spearheaded by Bob Willis and Ian Botham.

PETER WALKER *(Glamorgan and England)*: Playing for Glamorgan against Middlesex at Lord's in 1962, I was on the field for all of the three days' play bar about 45 minutes. I was pressed into service as an emergency opening batsman against an attack including England bowlers Alan Moss and Fred Titmus. I batted through the innings for an unbeaten 152 and then took seven for 58 with the new ball. Both performances were career bests. I made 18 in the second innings.

DOUG WALTERS *(New South Wales and Australia)*: The performance I'm happiest to recall was when I scored 242 in the first innings and 103 in the second for Australia against the West Indies in the fifth Test of the 1968–69 series at Sydney. My fourth-wicket partnership of 336 with skipper Bill Lawry in the first innings was a record for the series and in the second innings I became the first batsman to complete a double century and a century in the same Test. The West Indies had Wes Hall, Charlie Griffith, Garry Sobers, Clive Lloyd and Lance Gibbs in their attack so it was particularly pleasing to win the match by a record margin for the series of 382 runs.

JOHNNY WARDLE *(Yorkshire and England)*: England were playing South Africa on a hard, slow wicket at Newlands, Cape Town, on the 1956–57 tour. I had to work hard on skipper Peter May to convince him I would be better off bowling my wristy deliveries rather than the steadier orthodox style. By the time I had taken five for 53 in the first innings and seven for 36 in the second innings, Peter had come round to my way of thinking!

WASIM BARI *(Pakistan International Airways and Pakistan)*: I equalled the Test wicket-keeping record when holding eight catches for India against England at Headingley in 1971 and to make it even more memorable I managed to score 63 runs in our first innings. It was touch and go whether we would win the match but, just when success seemed in sight, John Lever took three wickets in four balls to lift England to victory by 25 runs.

ALLAN WATKINS *(Glamorgan and England)*: England started the second innings against India in the 1951 Test in Delhi 215 runs behind and staring defeat in the face. I batted nine hours for 138 and was not out at the end of the match with England 368 for six and we had salavaged a draw. I have never been so tired and weak-kneed as at the close.

PETER WILLEY *(Northamptonshire, Leicestershire and England)*: We were struggling at 92 for nine in the fifth Test at The Oval against the West Indies in 1980 when last man Bob Willis joined me at the wicket. Holding, Croft and Garner had shared the wickets amongst them and with 268 minutes to play England's lead was 197 which was looking an easy target for the West Indians. But Bob and I got our heads down and put together a partnership that frustrated the West Indies and saved the match for England. Bob batted with tremendous character and concentration and was unbeaten on 24 at the close. What made it so satisfying for me is that I was not out at 100, my maiden Test century, and to cap it all I won the Man of the Match award.

BOB WILLIS *(Surrey, Warwickshire and England)*: There was that never-to-be-forgotten 1981 Test against Australia at Headingley when 'Both' did his thing with the bat and I managed to take eight second-innings wickets for 43. But equal to that is the memory of coming back to play in the first Test against the West Indies at Trent Bridge in 1980 after being written off by many Fleet Street experts. I had the satisfaction of taking nine wickets in the match.

DON WILSON *(Yorkshire and England)*: One of the great memories of my life as a bowler is my one and only first-class century! It was for MCC against South Zone at Hyderabad on the 1963–64 tour. I went in to join Ken Barrington as night-watchman. We put on 200 together and I surpassed myself with a score of 112. Not bad for a left-arm slow bowling specialist.

BOB WOOLMER *(Kent and England)*: England followed on 341 runs behind Australia in the fourth Test at The Oval in 1975. I went in at number five and was at the wicket for eight and a quarter hours in scoring 149 runs. It was the slowest century of the England-Australia series and we held out for a draw. We scored 538 which was England's highest second-innings total against Australia.

DOUG WRIGHT *(Kent and England)*: I was playing for Kent against Somerset at Bath in 1939 and took eight for 35 in the first innings and eight for 45 in the second. Somerset's mighty hitter Arthur Wellard, who specialised in hitting sixes, was the only batsman to hold us up in their second innings with a score of 48 but he really lived dangerously and in the course of five of my deliveries we missed getting him out four times. Heavy rain on the final day robbed us of victory and the match finished in a draw.

SECTION FOUR
BEST OF THE REST

Seventy-five Test cricketers recall the greatest performance they've seen

BATTING

DENNIS AMISS *(Warwickshire and England)*: The innings that sticks in my mind is Lawrence Rowe's treble century for the West Indies against England in the third Test in Barbados in 1974. Even though he made us work hard in the field it was a pleasure to watch him making his strokes all round the wicket. He was at the wicket for just over ten hours and was always in command with some superb shots. I also remember the match for the fact that there were 99 'no balls' called, a Test record.

BOB BARBER *(Lancashire, Warwickshire and England)*: I recall a majestic innings of 174 by Peter May for Surrey against Lancashire at Old Trafford in 1958. His driving, in particular, was pure class. I would have applauded each shot if I hadn't been so busy chasing the ball! It was a sparkling gem of a knock, appreciated by everybody lucky enough to have seen it.

IAN BOTHAM *(Somerset and England)*: There are so many that I can choose from the gallery of great performances by my favourite batsman Viv Richards. The one I'll settle for is his 291 for West Indies against England at The Oval in 1976. He totally dominated the England attack and produced a procession of magnificent shots. He hammered 38 fours and this knock brought his record total of Test runs in a calendar year to a mind-blowing

1,710. Happily, I was not on the receiving end. He was in the sort of mood to murder any bowler's averages.

GEOFF BOYCOTT *(Yorkshire and England)*: I have to agree with Dennis Amiss. The best innings I've seen from another batsman was Lawrence Rowe's 302 for the West Indies in the third Test in Barbados in 1974. He batted for 612 minutes and hit a six and 36 fours. It was a beautifully constructed innings that was appreciated by all the England players and it was the first treble century by a West Indian batsman against England.

MIKE BREARLEY *(Middlesex and England)*: Like Ian Botham, I have to go for a Viv Richards innings. There are so many I have applauded but if I have to be tied down to one it would have to be his match-winning 138 not out for West Indies against England in the 1979 Prudential World Cup Final. I speak from painful experience when I say that he can make it almost impossible to set a field against him.

BRIAN CLOSE *(Yorkshire, Somerset and England)*: I have seen some magnificent batting over the years, particularly from Len Hutton and the exciting Vivian Richards. However, I think the best knock I ever saw was by Australian opener Arthur Morris for New South Wales against MCC during our 1950–51 tour. It was at Sydney and I remember him punishing us with a wide variety of shots on the way to a double century.

DENIS COMPTON *(Middlesex and England)*: I will never forget Stan McCabe's magnificent 232 for Australia against England at Trent Bridge in 1938. I caught him off Hedley Verity's bowling but not before he had severely punished our attack with shots to all parts of the ground. My fingers stung for hours after catching him because he really let fly at the ball.

COLIN COWDREY *(Kent and England)*: Denis Compton's 158 for England against South Africa at Old Trafford in 1955 is an innings that remains prominent in my memory. He produced every stroke in his vast repertoire, much to the despair of the bowlers. It was a magic innings in which Denis revealed the dashing style that made him such a hero when I was a youngster. He went to the wicket with a bat borrowed at the last minute from Fred Titmus. It was a battered old thing but in Denis's hands it was like a Stradivarius in the hands of Yehudi Menuhin! He simply stroked the ball around the ground.

MIKE DENNESS *(Kent, Essex and England)*: The innings that stands out in my memory was a classic century by Doug Walters for Australia against England in the second Test of the 1974–75 tour. He completed his 100 between tea and the close on the second day with a six off the last ball. That was real style.

TED DEXTER *(Sussex and England)*: M. J. K. (Mike) Smith produced a marvellous innings in the Gentlemen v. the Players match at Lord's in 1959. He scored 79 in the first innings and followed this with 166 in the second innings on a broken pitch that gave most of the other batsmen, myself included, terrible problems. His second innings knock, including 25 fours, was as good as anything you could hope to see and earned him a place a week later in the Old Trafford Test against India during which he scored his maiden Test century.

BILL EDRICH *(Middlesex and England)*: I have to go along with my old partner Denis Compton in selecting Stan McCabe's 232 for Australia against England at Trent Bridge in 1938. This was the innings when skipper Don Bradman summoned his team from the dressing-room and told them: 'Don't miss a single ball. You'll never see batting to equal it.' McCabe scored 232 out of 300 in under four hours!

JOHN EDRICH *(Surrey and England)*: Garry Sobers scored a magnificent century in the second innings of the second Test against England at Sabina Park, Jamaica, in 1968. We had forced the West Indies to follow on for the second successive Test after John Snow had dismissed Sobers' first ball, exactly as he had done the last time they had faced each other. But Garry had the last laugh with an unbeaten 113 in the second innings that saved the match for the West Indies. What made it so memorable was that huge cracks appeared in the wicket and at one end the ball either went along the ground or took off. Despite the unpredictable movement, Garry was in complete command. It was an eventful match all round, with play being held up on the fourth day by a bottle-throwing riot after Basil Butcher had been caught behind by Jim Parks off the bowling of Basil D'Oliveira.

KEITH FLETCHER *(Essex and England)*: There are so many magic moments from Garry Sobers that remain in the memory. I particularly recall his 183 for the Rest of the World against England at Lord's in 1973. He hit one six and 30 fours and gave a marvellous exhibition of violent yet controlled batting that revealed just why he is a legend in the game.

MIKE GATTING *(Middlesex and England)*: It has to be Ian Botham's astonishing 149 not out for England against Australia at Headingley in 1981. Nobody who saw it will ever forget it because not only was it a great exhibition of devastating hitting but it also transformed a game in which England looked doomed to defeat. A lot of Ian's shots would not be found in any textbook but there was no disputing how effective they were as tired Australian fielders kept retrieving the ball from the boundary. Another batsman I would like to mention is Kim Hughes, who batted on all five days of the Centenary Test against England at Lord's in 1980. He scored 117 and 84 in two knocks that were rich with fine stroke play and earned him the Man of the Match award.

SUNIL GAVASKAR *(Bombay, Somerset and England)*: There are two Test match innings by Indian team-mates that I feel deserve special mention. The first was by G. R. (Gundappa) Viswanath against New Zealand at Christchurch in 1976. He showed tremendous discipline and courage in scoring 83 in difficult conditions in the first innings of a drawn match. He was at the wicket for nearly three hours and hit ten fours with those beautiful wristy shots at which he specialises. In 1983, Mohinder Amarnath conjured 91 runs against the West Indian pace attack of Holding, Roberts, Garner and Marshall in the first innings of the fourth Test in Barbados. He hooked sixes off Holding, Roberts and Marshall during a stay of 203 minutes that deserved the reward of a century. It was batting at its best.

GRAHAM GOOCH *(Essex and England)*: The innings that left the biggest impression on me was Keith Fletcher's century for Essex against Middlesex at Southchurch Park, Southend, in 1977. Wayne Daniel was at his most hostile on a wearing and dangerous wicket. Keith was at the wicket for nearly five hours and gave an object lesson in technique and concentration. His score of 103 included 12 boundaries before he was caught by John Emburey off Mike Gatting's bowling. It was definitely the finest innings I've ever seen on a bad wicket.

DAVID GOWER *(Leicestershire and England)*: For drama and excitement, there can have been few innings to match Ian Botham's match-turning 149 not out against Australia at Headingley in 1981. The most cultured innings I've seen was Graeme Pollock scoring one of his innumerable centuries for Eastern Province against Western Province at Port Elizabeth in 1974–75. It was a pleasure watching a master at work.

TOM GRAVENEY *(Gloucester, Worcestershire and England)*: The tops for me was Neil Harvey's 92 not out for Australia against England in Sydney in 1954–55. It was a glittering performance, made all the more memorable because his team-mates were getting into all sorts of trouble against the pace of Frank Tyson who bowled faster than anybody I have ever seen. He was the only Australian batsman who offered any real resistance but he ran out of partners before he could reach a deserved ton. 'Typhoon' Tyson took six for 85 as Australia tumbled all out in their second innings for 184 and defeat by 38 runs.

KIM HUGHES *(Western Australia and Australia)*: I have never seen an innings quite like that which Viv Richards produced for the West Indies against Australia in a one-day international at Melbourne in 1979–80. He was given pain-killing injections before the match because of a back injury and hobbled throughout his stay at the wicket during which he scored an unbeaten 153 off just 131 balls. As I watched the power and genius that flowed from his bat I wondered to myself whether there has been a batsman from any era that could have produced a better performance. Somehow, I doubt it.

SIR LEN HUTTON *(Yorkshire and England)*: There are two innings that I recall above all others. The first was Don Bradman's 334 at Leeds in the third Test in 1930. He scored 309 runs on the first day which is a record I cannot imagine ever being beaten. His double century came up in just 214 minutes and I cannot remember any of his shots going above waist height. The other innings of which I have vivid memories is Walter Hammond's 242 runs for England against Australia at Lord's in 1938. It was a magnificent captain's innings, full of fluent strokes and superbly judged running.

IMRAN KHAN *(Lahore, Oxford University, Worcestershire, Sussex and Pakistan)*: Mohsin Khan compiled 70 runs when opening the batting for Pakistan against the West Indies in the Prudential World Cup semi-finals at The Oval in 1983. It was a damp and uneven wicket and Mohsin had to face the full blast of a pace attack that had

Garner, Holding, Roberts and Marshall sharing the bowling between them. It was a truly gutsy knock that also called for a lot of technique.

SYED KIRMANI *(Mysore and India)*: My choice is a remarkable all-round performance by Ian Botham in the Golden Jubilee Test at Bombay in 1980. He scored a sparkling century and took 13 wickets. It was a highly impressive demonstration of his great versatility and proved that he is a master with the bat and the ball.

TONY LEWIS *(Glamorgan and England)*: The innings I select is Majid Khan's unbeaten 156 out of a total of 256 all out for Glamorgan against Worcestershire at Sophia Gardens, Cardiff, in 1969. He produced a marvellous range of brilliant strokes on a broken wicket and against an excellent attack. It was one of several superb knocks from Majid for Glamorgan that season and his accumulation of 1,547 runs played a major part in our County Championship triumph.

BRIAN LUCKHURST *(Kent and England)*: I well remember Garry Sobers producing an astonishing one-man show for Notts against Kent in a County championship match at Dover in 1968. He was devastating with the ball, taking ten wickets in the match including seven for 69 in the first innings. Notts had to chase runs in their second innings and Sobers promoted himself in the order. He hammered an unbeaten 105 in 77 minutes to steer Notts to a seven-wicket victory with ten minutes to spare.

PETER MAY *(Surrey and England)*: Len Hutton produced a glorious innings of 205 against the West Indies in Kingston in the fifth and final Test of the 1953–54 tour. It was the first time an England captain had scored a double century in an overseas Test and it laid the foundation for a nine-wicket victory that squared the series. The match was also notable in that a young player called Garfield Sobers made his Test debut.

COLIN MILBURN *(Northamptonshire and England)*: Like John Edrich, I have not seen a better innings than the 113 not out by Garry Sobers for the West Indies against England at Kingston in 1968. He made his runs in majestic style on the worst Test wicket I have ever seen and against a very useful England attack.

ARTHUR MILTON *(Gloucestershire and England)*: The innings that has remained in my memory is the Neil Harvey knock of 167 for Australia against England at Melbourne in 1958–59. It was an innings rich with superb strokes and positive play. It was the first century by an Australian against England for 11 Tests and was a classic that set up the Aussies for a victory by eight wickets.

BRIAN ROSE *(Somerset and England)*: Viv Richards scored a controlled and brilliant 139 not out for Somerset against Warwickshire in the 1978 Gillette Cup at Taunton. We were chasing runs to win and Viv was under great pressure but he still managed to hit five sixes and ten fours, clinching a thrilling victory with a six-hit.

PHIL SHARPE *(Yorkshire, Derbyshire and England)*: I was thrilled as a youngster to see Len Hutton in full flow during a Scarborough Festival match. It was poetry in motion and the memory of his innings has remained with me ever since. He scored 241, showing superb technique and a full range of strokes.

MIKE SMITH *(Leicestershire, Warwickshire and England)*: I recall a classical innings by Colin Cowdrey for England against the West Indies at Sabina Park, Jamaica, in 1959–60. He scored 114 in his first innings but it was in his second-innings knock of 97 that he displayed really regal form. He and Geoff Pullar shared an opening stand of 117 that was magical to watch.

DAVID STEELE *(Northants, Derbyshire and England)*: The most impressive batting display I have ever seen came from Graeme Pollock when he scored 209 for South Africa against Australia in a Test match at Newlands, Cape Town. It was a magnificent innings from the powerful left-hander who was badly handicapped by a thigh muscle injury and had to play with a runner. He scored 209 out of 353 in 350 minutes.

DILIP VENGSARKAR *(Bombay and India)*: Sunil Gavaskar scored 205 runs on the first day of the first Test for India against West Indies at Bombay in 1978–79. He reached his double century in just over six hours, hitting two sixes and twenty-seven fours. It was a splendid exhibition of controlled aggression and he was always in command against a powerful West Indian attack.

PETER WALKER *(Glamorgan and England)*: Tom Graveney made an unbeaten 204 out of a total of 280 all out for Gloucestershire against Glamorgan at Newport in 1961. He scored his runs on a turning wicket and against top-quality off-spinners Don Shepherd and Jim McConnon, and he also made me suffer. As we went up the pavilion steps at the close of the innings, Wilf Wooller said, 'That's the worst 200 I've ever seen . . .!'

DOUG WALTERS *(New South Wales and Australia)*: Garfield Sobers gave a devastating display of batsmanship on his way to 250 runs for the Rest of the World against Australia at Melbourne in 1971–72. It was a commanding innings that revealed just why he is considered one of the finest cricketers of all time. He produced every shot in the book and also many of his own invention.

ALLAN WATKINS: Everton Weekes gave a thrilling exhibition of power shots and controlled glances while making 147 runs for the West Indies against Glamorgan at Swansea in 1950. It was wonderful entertainment for the crowd and even we players enjoyed it when we weren't chasing the ball to the boundary!

BOB WYATT *(Warwickshire, Worcestershire and England)*: I have never seen a better innings than that constructed by Stan McCabe for Australia against England at Trent Bridge in 1938. It was an absolutely splendid knock, full of imaginative and beautifully weighted strokes.

NORMAN YARDLEY *(Yorkshire and England)*: I plump for Denis Compton's 145 not out for England against Australia at Old Trafford in 1948. He was struck on the head early in his innings when attempting a mighty swipe off a bouncer for Ray Lindwall, who was bowling faster than anybody I had ever seen. Denis had to leave the field to receive medical attention and returned after being stitched and bandaged to play a real hero's innings.

PATRICK MOORE'S
DREAM TEAM

1 W. G. GRACE
2 JACK HOBBS
3 FRANK WORRELL
4 DONALD BRADMAN
5 DENIS COMPTON
6 DEREK RANDALL
7 LES AMES
8 RAY LINDWALL
9 SYDNEY BARNES
10 FREDERICK 'THE DEMON' SPOFFORTH
11 DOUG WRIGHT

'I was down with 'flu when making my selection, and it was such a difficult job that I suffered a relapse! I could have selected ten teams of equal strength and ability and it was sheer torture having to omit so many of my favourite players. As a village green leg-spinner I feel ill-qualified as a selector but I have done my best and ask for forgiveness from those great players whom I have reluctantly left out.'

PATRICK MOORE

PATRICK MOORE, world-respected astronomer, xylophonist extraordinary and popular television personality, has made an impact at many charity cricket matches with his considerable physical presence, his beguiling spin bowling and his somewhat eccentric batting.

BOWLING

DAVID ALLEN *(Gloucestershire and England)*: My selection is a joint spell of bowling by Fred Trueman and Brian Statham for England against the West Indies in Trinidad in 1959–60. The West Indies used seven bowlers without being able to get anything out of the lifeless wicket. But Fred and Brian gave a superb display of controlled swing and seam bowling in West Indies' second innings to lift England to victory by 256 runs. Fred took six wickets and Brian five.

GEOFF ARNOLD *(Surrey, Sussex and England)*: I have rarely seen pace to match that generated by Wayne Daniel for Middlesex against Sussex in the 1978 Benson & Hedges tournament. Bowling down the hill at Hove, he skittled six of us out for 17 runs and we were dismissed for 60. It was the fastest bowling I'd seen since facing Lillee and Thomson at their peak in Australia.

TREVOR BAILEY *(Essex and England)*: Jim Laker's 19 wickets for England against Australia in the 1956 Old Trafford Test was a unique performance that will never be equalled. Sitting in the dressing-room immediately afterwards, I said that I could not believe it had happened, and I still find it difficult.

JACK BIRKENSHAW *(Yorkshire, Leicestershire, Worcestershire and England)*: Paddy Clift took eight for 17 with a brilliant spell of medium-pace bowling for Leicestershire against MCC at Lord's in a dramatic opening match of the 1976 season. It was his first game as a fully qualified Leicestershire player after coming over from Rhodesia. Thanks to his bowling, we dismissed MCC for 149 on a pitch that gave little assistance to the bowlers. We declared our second innings closed at 226 for two and looked in a strong position, with MCC needing 325 to win in four and a half hours. Then Dennis Amiss and Mike

Brearley turned the game upside down with a 301 opening stand and they reached their victory target for the loss of one wicket and with ten minutes to spare! So Paddy Clift found himself on the losing side despite producing the best bowling performance I have ever seen.

ALEC BEDSER *(Surrey and England)*: A single over by Ray Lindwall stands out in my memory. He was playing for the Australian tourists against Surrey at The Oval. I recall him bowling six balls to Peter May that were as close as you can get to perfection. Every ball was perfectly pitched and each of them was a vicious outswinger. Even a batsman of Peter's outstanding quality was made to look distinctly uncomfortable by Lindwall's pace and accuracy.

BILL BOWES *(Yorkshire and England)*: There has in my experience been nothing to match Hedley Verity's ten wickets for ten runs for Yorkshire against Notts at Leeds in 1932. It was a magnificent performance heightened by the fact that the bowler at the other end was the redoubtable George Macaulay who was trying his hardest to claim a victim even when Hedley had taken his ninth wicket.

DAVID BROWN *(Warwickshire and England)*: John Snow's seven for 49 against the West Indies at Sabina Park, Jamaica, on the 1967–68 tour takes some beating. He bowled some devastating stuff and had the distinction of getting Garry Sobers out first ball for the second time in successive innings.

TOM CARTWRIGHT *(Warwickshire, Somerset, Glamorgan and England)*: Alec Bedser wrecked Warwickshire with eight for 18 for Surrey in a County Championship match at The Oval in 1953. That was the season in which Alec did so much to help England regain the Ashes. He continually reproduced the swinging form he showed against us at The Oval throughout the Test series.

GODFREY EVANS *(Kent and England)*: Jim Laker's 19 wickets for England against the Aussies at Old Trafford in 1956 has to come out top. I only managed to get in on his act once, when I stumped Ron Archer. He tied the Aussie batsmen in knots and they found him just unplayable. I also recall with some relish Trevor Bailey's seven for 34 against the West Indies in Jamaica in 1954 and Frank Tyson's seven for 27 that lifted England to victory against Australia in Melbourne in 1955.

ALF GOVER *(Surrey and England)*: Like Godfrey, I have an outstanding memory of Frank Tyson at his fastest and fiercest in Australia on the 1954–55 tour. His seven for 27 in 12.3 overs at Melbourne was fast bowling at its most hostile and spectacular.

RAY ILLINGWORTH *(Yorkshire, Leicestershire and England)*: John Snow claimed seven Australian wickets for 40 runs in the second innings of the fourth Test in Sydney on our 1970–71 tour. His brilliant bowling helped us achieve England's biggest victory over the Aussies in more than 30 years. We won by 299 runs. John bowled as well as any fast bowler I have ever seen during that tour. Few batsmen in the world could have played him with the new ball. He got chest-high bounce from only just short of a length, got movement off the pitch and, above all, he bowled a beautiful line. Time and again he pitched the ball fractionally outside the off stump so that if it did even a little bit he had the batsman in trouble.

ROBIN JACKMAN *(Surrey and England)*: It's easy to recall a devastating spell by Surrey off-spinner Pat Pocock against Sussex at Eastbourne in 1972. He was virtually unplayable and took seven wickets in 11 deliveries: four in successive balls, five in six balls, six in nine and finishing with seven in 11. Five wickets fell in his final over, four of them bowled and the other run out. The seven wickets in his last two overs cost him just four runs!

ALAN KNOTT *(Kent and England)*: Michael Holding's 14 wickets for the West Indies against England in the fifth Test at The Oval in 1976 was the most impressive fast bowling I've ever seen. The best spin-bowling performance came from Derek Underwood for Kent against Sussex at Hastings in 1973. He had the batsmen mesmerised and took eight wickets for nine runs in 10.1 overs.

JIM LAKER *(Surrey, Essex and England)*: I will always remember Johnny Wardle's seven wickets for 36 for England against South Africa at Cape Town in 1956–57. He switched from his natural leg breaks to a mixture of 'chinamen' and googlies. His variety, control and accuracy was quite remarkable. South Africa were all out for 72 and England won by 312 runs.

DAVID LARTER *(Northamptonshire and England)*: Wes Hall produced the best demonstration of controlled fast bowling that I have seen when taking four wickets for the West Indies against England in the second innings of the 1963 Lord's Test. Hall bowled throughout the 200 minutes of play that was possible on the last day. He produced a sustained spell of hostile and accurate bowling that, for spectacle and stamina, takes some beating. His final figures of four for 93 do not do justice to his magnificent display.

JOHN LEVER *(Essex and England)*: Dennis Lillee's 11 wickets for Australia against England in the Centenary Test in Melbourne in 1977 was the greatest bowling performance I have witnessed. I was one of his victims when he took six for 26 in the first innings and can vouch for the fact that his bowling was as close as you can get to perfection. His line and length and movement of the ball either into or away from the bat was always deadly accurate and his pace was just phenomenal.

DENNIS LILLEE *(Western Australia and Australia)*: The stand-out memory for me is Bob Massie's astonishing Test debut for Australia against England in the second Test at Lord's in 1972. He took eight for 84 in the first innings and then eight for 53 in the second innings to send England tumbling to an eight-wicket defeat. The conditions were humid and he swung the ball around as if he had it attached to a piece of string.

RODNEY MARSH *(Western Australia and Australia)*: For me, the best bowling I've ever seen was Dennis Lillee's explosive performance against England in the 1977 Centenary Test at Melbourne. He proved that he is the No 1 bowler in the world with a sustained display of hostile yet controlled pace that had the England batsmen in all sorts of trouble. In my opinion, 'D. K.' should have been Man of the Match ahead of Derek Randall.

ARTHUR McINTYRE *(Surrey and England)*: Peter Loader took nine for 28 for Surrey against Kent at Blackheath in 1953. It was one of those days when he could do no wrong and every ball was spot-on. We were willing him to get the ten wickets he deserved but the last batsman was run out.

JOHN MURRAY *(Middlesex and England)*: Richie Benaud gave a match-winning performance when he took six for 70 in England's second innings at Old Trafford in 1961. His bowling ensured that Australia would retain the Ashes. Ted Dexter had been going like a train but Richie took command by switching to round the wicket and pitching consistently into the rough. It was a masterly exhibition of controlled bowling.

JIM PARKS *(Sussex, Somerset and England)*: Jack Walsh, Leicestershire's Australian-born slow left-arm specialist bowler, baffled the batsmen of Sussex – me included – with his 'chinamen' and googlies in 1952. He took eight wickets in each innings. It was sheer wizardry.

PAT POCOCK *(Surrey and England)*: Like Alan Knott, I go for Michael Holding's 14 wickets for the West Indies against England at The Oval in 1976. He managed to produce incredible pace on one of the slowest of all wickets. Viv Richards laid the foundation for a West Indies victory with a marvellous innings of 291. Then Holding took over, taking eight for 92 in the first innings and six for 57 in the second innings.

JOHN PRICE *(Middlesex and England)*: England were playing South Africa at Lord's in June, 1955. I was lucky enough to have finished my 'A-levels' and so took a day off school. I had the unforgettable pleasure of seeing Brian Statham bowl all day long while taking seven for 39. It was a treat to watch a bowling master in action.

MIKE SELVEY *(Surrey, Middlesex and England)*: Along with Alan Knott and Pat Pocock, I select Michael Holding's performance for West Indies against England at The Oval in 1976 as the best bowling display I have ever seen. He kept up tremendous pressure on the England batsmen and finished with a haul of 14 wickets on a dead slow wicket.

DEREK SHACKLETON *(Hampshire and England)*: There has been nothing better than Jim Laker's 19 wickets for England against Australia at Old Trafford in 1956. It was an absolutely stunning display of controlled spin and flight variations. The fact that Tony Lock operating at the opposite end could take only one wicket speaks volumes for the quality of Laker's performance.

ALAN SMITH *(Warwickshire and England)*: Dennis Lillee, my idea of the perfect bowler, confirmed my opinion of his ability in the Centenary Test in Melbourne in 1977 when he took 11 wickets in the match for 165. He showed exceptional stamina and tremendous competitive drive and this, allied to his great pace and accuracy, added up to yet another of his match-winning performances for Australia.

JOHN SNOW *(Sussex, Warwickshire and England)*: Like the great Dennis Lillee, I choose Bob Massie's 16 wickets for Australia against England at Lord's in 1972. It was a sensational Test debut and a mind-blowing experience. Perhaps it literally was a mind-blowing effort because Bob never again seemed quite the same force. He took eight for 84 in the first innings and eight for 53 in the second innings to finish with incredible match figures of 16 for 137. His analysis is a record for any bowler in his first Test match and for any Test at Lord's. Only Jim Laker and Sydney Barnes have ever taken more wickets in a Test. This bowling performance plus a knock of 131 by Greg Chappell lifted Australia to victory by eight wickets. Not surprisingly, it has become known as 'Massie's Match'.

BRIAN STATHAM *(Lancashire and England)*: It has to be Jim Laker's 19 wickets against Australia at Old Trafford in 1956. My contribution was taking a skied catch off Richie Benaud. The wicket was never a bad one at any time. It turned a bit but slowly and there was no lift. It was a wonderful performance considering that the talented Tony Lock at the other end could claim only one wicket.

ROY TATTERSALL *(Lancashire and England)*: Like so many cricketers of my generation, I would have to pick Jim Laker's 19 wickets in the 1956 Old Trafford Test against Australia. I can't believe this performance will ever be bettered, especially in Test cricket.

FRED TITMUS *(Middlesex, Surrey and England)*: Fred Trueman would tell me that the best bowling performance I have ever seen is one of his displays – and, of course, he would be right! Fred not only *talks* a good game of cricket. He could play it as well. I particularly recall his 12 wickets for 119 against the West Indies at Edgbaston in 1963. His last six wickets came in a blistering 24-ball spell which cost him just one scoring stroke by Lance Gibbs. Thanks to Fred, we won by 217 runs.

ROGER TOLCHARD *(Leicestershire and England)*: Graham 'Garth' McKenzie had a memorable spell for Leicestershire in 1971 when he took seven wickets for eight runs and sent Glamorgan tumbling all out for 24. They were eight wickets down for just 11 runs when I had a legitimate catch behind the stumps turned down, so Graham's figures could have been even better!

FRED TRUEMAN *(Yorkshire, Derbyshire and England)*: My old partner Brian Statham took 11 for 97 for England against South Africa in the 1960 Lord's Test. He kept a superb line and length throughout the match and was mainly responsible for England's comfortable victory by an innings and 73 runs.

DEREK UNDERWOOD *(Kent and England)*: I'll always remember Tony Greig taking 13 wickets for 156 runs for England against the West Indies in Trinidad on the 1973–74 tour. It was something of a freak bowling effort when he was helped by his height (6ft 7in), the unpredictable bounce of the ball and the fact that so many of the batsmen facing him were left-handed. I also recall the match for Geoff Boycott's disciplined batting when he failed by just one run to score a century in each innings.

BILL VOCE *(Nottinghamshire and England)*: I have never seen fast bowling to match that produced by Harold Larwood against Australia in the first Test in Sydney on the 1932–33 tour. An indication of how quickly the ball was coming off the bat is that there were six of us in the slips and we dropped six catches between us during one of his morning spells. We won the match by ten wickets and Harold took ten for 124. It was devastating stuff.

JOHNNY WARDLE *(Yorkshire and England)*: We went into the Trent Bridge Test against Australia in 1953 with only four recognised bowlers, and so big Alec Bedser was carrying a lot of responsibility on his wide shoulders. Our job as support bowlers was to contain the Aussies while Alec concentrated on trying to get them out on a good wicket but in poor light. Evidence that he did his job to perfection is that he took 14 wickets for 99 runs. Rain prevented us getting the victory that Alec's performance so richly deserved and the match ended in a draw. We had the consolation of regaining the Ashes at the end of a series in which Alec was an outstanding success.

BOB WILLIS *(Surrey, Warwickshire and England)*: Like so many other people privileged to have seen the performance, I select Michael Holding's 14 wickets for the West Indies against England on a featherbed wicket at The Oval in 1976. It was an exceptional demonstration of the art of fast bowling.

DON WILSON *(Yorkshire and England)*: One over from Michael Holding has remained in my memory. It was his first over to Geoff Boycott for West Indies against England at Bridgetown in 1981. I have never seen a more hostile over and only a batsman of Boycott's quality could have survived to the final ball which knocked out his off stump.

DOUG WRIGHT *(Kent and England)*: There are so many outstanding performances that I could choose, with any of several remarkable performances by my former Kent colleague 'Tich' Freeman topping the bill. Three times in successive years, he took all ten wickets in a match for Kent and he regularly took more than 250 wickets in a season.

SECTION FIVE
THE SPORTSMEN'S SPORTSMEN

Seventy-five Test stars name their favourite
non-cricketing sportsmen

DAVID ALLEN *(Gloucestershire and England)*
RAY REARDON is my particular favourite. Not only is he
master of his sport but he conducts himself in a way that
gives snooker as well as himself a good image.

DENNIS AMISS *(Warwickshire and England)*
KEVIN KEEGAN who always appears to have done the
right things at the right time on and off the football pitch.
He is a great competitor and when I have been in his
company I have been impressed by his demeanour. He
always has time to listen to others and is unspoiled by his
great success.

GEOFF ARNOLD *(Surrey, Sussex and England)*
JACK NICKLAUS. As a bit of a golfer myself, I admire
his single-minded concentration and his total dedication.
He has the ability to play the shot required and to wipe
from his mind what has gone before. There are also a lot
of footballers I admire and envy because I would dearly
have loved to have been a professional footballer.

TREVOR BAILEY *(Essex and England)*
TOM FINNEY, the Preston and England international
who was the *complete* footballer. Although best remembered as a winger, he was equally effective in any forward
position and apart from being a gifted player was also a
true sportsman.

BOB BARBER *(Lancashire, Warwickshire and England)*
Lawn tennis ace *PANCHO GONZALES,* for his wonderful skill and athleticism. He was like a panther on the court, mixing power, skill and inventiveness into a marvellous all-round game.

ALEC BEDSER *(Surrey and England)*
ARNOLD PALMER is somebody I have always admired. He has personality appeal, is prepared to take a risk and continually shows a great respect for the traditions of his game. He has wonderful self-discipline and his behaviour on and off the golf course serves as an ideal example for all sports participants and followers.

IAN BOTHAM *(Somerset and England)*
JOHN McENROE, who apart from being a richly talented tennis player is also an exceptionally competitive character who will never concede second best.

GEOFF BOYCOTT *(Yorkshire and England)*
My favourite sports away from cricket are lawn tennis and golf and the sportsmen I most identify with are *ROD LAVER and BJORN BORG and JACK NICKLAUS and GARY PLAYER.* They are all fine ambassadors for their sport and never give anything less than 100 per cent.

DAVID BROWN *(Warwickshire and England)*
JACK NICKLAUS has my total admiration. He has proved that you can be the best in the world at your sport and yet still behave as the perfect sporting gent.

TOM CARTWRIGHT *(Warwickshire, Somerset, Glamorgan and England)*
BRIAN CLOUGH, who is honest, good for all professional sportsmen and his achievements are almost unparalleled. His outstanding performances have not been confined just to management. It is sometimes forgotten that he was one of the game's most consistent goal scorers until injury forced a premature retirement.

BRIAN CLOSE *(Yorkshire, Somerset and England)*
I admire a lot of sportsmen, not because of their prowess but because they are *men*. The qualities I appreciate are skill, consideration to others, loyalty, toughness, intelligence and maturity. *JACK NICKLAUS and LESTER PIGGOTT* are two who spring to mind as having these qualities.

DENIS COMPTON *(Middlesex and England)*
Golfer *GARY PLAYER* is the sportsman I most admire. He was not born with the greatest natural talent for his game but achieved greatness through sheer dedication.

COLIN COWDREY *(Kent and England)*
ARNOLD PALMER and PETER THOMSON share my admiration. They have complete mastery of their sport, are totally dedicated, perfectly mannered and scrupulously fair sportsmen. Their enjoyment while playing their game permeates to everyone lucky to see them in action.

MIKE DENNESS *(Kent, Essex and England)*
JACK NICKLAUS as a supreme golfer and dignified champion . . .
JACKIE STEWART, for his brilliance behind the wheel.

TED DEXTER *(Sussex and England)*
National Hunt jockey *JOHN FRANCOME,* a brave man in a tough sport who treats it all without fuss and has a smile for everyone.

BILL EDRICH *(Middlesex and England)*
SIR ROGER BANNISTER, for proving that the 'impossible' was possible when breaking the four-minute mile barrier in 1954. Many have since followed him but nobody can ever take away the fact that he was the first.

JOHN EDRICH *(Surrey and England)*
I am not a racing man but I admire the way *LESTER PIGGOTT* goes about things. Day in and day out he

shows tremendous discipline and he has an incredible desire to win, especially on the big occasions when it really matters.

GODFREY EVANS *(Kent and England)*
HENRY COOPER, completely unspoiled by his success. A credit to his sport and country, both in and out of the ring.

KEITH FLETCHER *(Essex and England)*
JACK NICKLAUS and LEE TREVINO, not only for their ability on the golf course but also for the way they conduct themselves in public. There's something about top-tournament golfers like Nicklaus and Trevino that sets them apart from other sportsmen. They are always so easy to talk to and cope with all the pressures with such confidence.

SUNIL GAVASKAR *(Bombay, Somerset and India)*
PRAKASH PADUKONE, who is India's badminton champion. He won the All-England championship in 1980. I admire all sportsmen who can keep their cool in moments of stress because I myself find difficulty in doing so.

GRAHAM GOOCH *(Essex and England)*
BOBBY CHARLTON, who when playing for England and Manchester United was a great sportsman as well as a great footballer. He never used to argue with officials and gave the perfect example to youngsters in how to conduct themselves in the sports arena.

DAVID GOWER *(Leicestershire and England)*
I admire all those who manage to play their sports with flair and enjoyment, yet with control. If I have to be pinned down to naming names perhaps I should mention golfers such as *SEVERIANO BALLESTEROS and GREG NORMAN* as coming into the category.

TOM GRAVENEY *(Gloucestershire, Worcestershire and England)*
BILL BEAUMONT, for what he achieved for English rugby . . . the perfection of *STEVE DAVIS* at the snooker table . . . the superb golf commentaries of *PETER ALLISS . . .* and *BOBBY CHARLTON's* sportsmanship in a hard game.

KIM HUGHES *(Western Australia and Australia)*
JIMMY CONNORS, who is completely natural on court and is not afraid of getting excited. He exudes a genuine love and enjoyment of his sport which is not always the way with so many sports stars today.

SIR LEN HUTTON *(Yorkshire and England)*
HENRY COTTON as an excellent golfer and **BEN HOGAN** as a marvellous golfer and incredibly brave man. It was a miracle that Hogan played again after a car crash that nearly killed him.

RAY ILLINGWORTH *(Yorkshire, Leicestershire and England)*
TOM FINNEY, who was not only an absolutely brilliant footballer but also a gentleman and sportsman on and off the pitch.

IMRAN KHAN *(Lahore, Oxford University, Worcestershire, Sussex and Pakistan)*
MUHAMMAD ALI, who made a barbaric sport like boxing into an art. He is also an immensely articulate man with a sharp wit, a rarity in that field.

DOUG INSOLE *(Essex and England)*
JOE MERCER, football's favourite 'uncle' whose approach to the game both as a player and manager has been exemplary – constructive, courageous, entertaining, sportsmanlike, which is the same image he projects as a man.

SYED KIRMANI *(Mysore and India)*
There are two who I admire the most: **MUHAMMAD ALI,** the greatest boxer who always provided action to go with his words; **PELE,** the Black Pearl of soccer for his tremendous control on the ball.

ROBIN JACKMAN *(Surrey and England)*
Golfer **GARY PLAYER,** for his dedication to both his sport and his country. He is a real battler who never concedes defeat until the final putt. The way in which he came from behind to win the US Masters at the age of 42 in 1978 typified the way he has always produced 100 per cent effort and enormous willpower.

ALAN KNOTT *(Kent and England)*
PAT JENNINGS, the Arsenal and Northern Ireland goal-keeper. If I had been six inches taller, I would have loved to have been a goalkeeper. What an example Pat gives youngsters. He is highly competitive, yet perfectly con-trolled and he has a wonderful balance that is not easy to acquire.

JIM LAKER *(Surrey, Essex and England)*
JACK NICKLAUS, who is the greatest ever golfer yet appears never to have changed his manner, outlook, charm and modesty since he won his first major tourna-ment some 25 years ago.

DAVID LARTER *(Northamptonshire and England)*
Shot putter **GEOFF CAPES,** who battled very successfully against the odds throughout his career and managed to stay at the top in his sport.

JOHN LEVER *(Essex and England)*
BJORN BORG, for his fitness, stamina, skill and incre-dible consistency, particularly at Wimbledon.

TONY LEWIS *(Glamorgan and England)*
DICKIE JEEPS, the former England rugby international. He was a fine player and is now a direct and positive administrator and leader as chairman of the Sports Council and President of the Rugby Football Union.

DENNIS LILLEE *(Western Australia and Australia)*
MUHAMMAD ALI, who was the complete athlete and somebody who brought his skill, power and charm to the attention of the world.

DAVID LLOYD *(Lancashire and England)*
JOE JORDAN, who used to play for 'The Reds'. Needless to say I am a Manchester United supporter and Joe always gave them 100 per cent in effort and determination.

BRIAN LUCKHURST (Kent and England)
GARY PLAYER, for his dedication and for always representing his sport and country with dignity and style.

RODNEY MARSH *(Western Australia and Australia)*
JACK NICKLAUS, who has proved himself a *great* golfer over three decades. His ability has stood the test of time.

PETER MAY *(Surrey and England)*
JACK NICKLAUS, for his dedication and deportment over so many years during which he has been a wonderful ambassador for his sport both on and off the golf course.

COLIN MILBURN *(Northamptonshire and England)*
I love all sports and like to see characters who have charisma to go with their talent. **MUHAMMAD ALI** was the king. I wonder where boxing would have gone in the last 20 years without his mass appeal?

ARTHUR MILTON *(Gloucestershire and England)*
LESTER PIGGOTT, for sheer dedication and talent, plus his tremendous discipline with his diet. He is not apt to

open his mouth too much but he is worth listening to when he does.

ARTHUR McINTYRE *(Surrey and England)*
JACK NICKLAUS. Even after the success and fame he has achieved he still gives the impression of being a gentleman and a fine sportsman. He has set a wonderful example of how champions should conduct themselves at all times.

JOHN MURRAY *(Middlesex and England)*
JACK NICKLAUS, who does not allow his great desire to win to override his enjoyment or the traditions of the game which are equally important to him.

ALAN OAKMAN *(Sussex and England)*
Former world snooker champion *FRED DAVIS,* who in a very professional and competitive sport always appears to be enjoying himself and this is conveyed to the audience. You don't often see this refreshing attitude in modern sport.

JIM PARKS *(Sussex, Somerset and England)*
JACK NICKLAUS. I admire his terrific swing and the sheer power of his game. He appears so natural and completely unaffected by all the world-wide success he has enjoyed for so many years.

PAT POCOCK *(Surrey and England)*
Former world motor racing champion *JACKIE STE-WART.* Throughout his dedicated career he always remained a very human person, mindful of others. He consistently gave a magnificent account of himself whatever he tackled (and continues to do so).

JOHN PRICE *(Middlesex and England)*
Golfer *JACK NICKLAUS* and Rugby players *GARETH EDWARDS and BARRY JOHN,* all of them supreme

179

artists who have been true sportsmen even when the pressures they have faced have been at a peak.

PETER RICHARDSON *(Worcestershire, Kent and England)*
JACK NICKLAUS, the perfect professional sportsman. His game has withstood all challenges and competition for many years. As a person he has continually silenced his 'knockers' with grace, charm and style.

BRIAN ROSE *(Somerset and England)*
Golfer *TOM WATSON,* a model professional who has a great temperament to go with his talent. He is a born winner but never brags about his performances. He just gets on with playing the game to the best of his ability.

DEREK SHACKLETON *(Hampshire and England)*
KEVIN KEEGAN. He is not only a talented footballer and good sportsman but his public image is a credit to him. He sets a fine example for youngsters.

PHIL SHARPE *(Yorkshire, Derbyshire and England)*
JACK NICKLAUS, a great golfer and, I am told, 'nice with it'. He is a wonderful ambassador for both his sport and his country.

REG SIMPSON *(Nottinghamshire and England)*
I admire the athletes who are dedicated to their sport and training. I am thinking of Olympic champions like *SE-BASTIAN COE, STEVE OVETT, DALEY THOMPSON* and *ALLAN WELLS.*

ALAN SMITH *(Warwickshire and England)*
JACK NICKLAUS, who has been utterly pleasant while becoming the world's best golfer. He has the ability to concentrate but never at the expense of forgetting to acknowledge the galleries that follow him around the fairways of the world.

MIKE SMITH *(Leicestershire, Warwickshire and England)*
BILL BEAUMONT, the former England rugby captain, for his integrity and performance. He never gave less than 100 per cent and was a master at motivating the players around him.

JOHN SNOW *(Sussex, Warwickshire and England)*
JOE BLOGGS, representing the fanatics who play for love come rain or shine. They have my total admiration. I don't think I could ever do it, though I suppose I must have done it at some time early in my career.

BRIAN STATHAM *(Lancashire and England)*
BJORN BORG, who at his peak was not only extremely talented but got on with playing the game without resorting to emotional, bad-tempered outbursts. He set an example in the way he accepted decisions without dissent and remained cool and calm under the severest pressure. His Wimbledon record is quite extraordinary and proves that he had great powers of concentration to go with his ability.

DICK SPOONER *(Warwickshire and England)*
JACK NICKLAUS, for his great application to golf and his unassuming manner despite being the world's No 1 at his sport. He sets a behaviour pattern for all champions.

ROY TATTERSALL *(Lancashire and England)*
TOM FINNEY, a great, two-footed footballer who could play in any forward position. He was modest, loyal, sporting and a wonderful example to all other sportsmen.

BOB TAYLOR *(Derbyshire and England)*
JACK NICKLAUS, for his consistency, dedication, will-to-win temperament and his gentlemanly behaviour. He has been at the top in his sport for nearly a quarter of a century and has always given of his best.

FRED TITMUS *(Middlesex, Surrey and England)*
Golfer *LEE TREVINO*. He is the perfect pro and also manages to entertain while displaying his great talent on the greens and the fairways of the world.

ROGER TOLCHARD *(Leicestershire and England)*
MUHAMMAD ALI, a magnificient champion at his peak who was ten years ahead of his time . . . *GARY PLAYER,* a great but fair competitor whose record in the major golf championships speaks volumes for his ability and application.

FRED TRUEMAN *(Yorkshire, Derbyshire and England)*
MUHAMMAD ALI. He kept telling the world that he was 'The Greatest' and then went into the ring and proved just that.

DEREK UNDERWOOD *(Kent and England)*
Olympic champions like *SEBASTIAN COE, STEVE OVETT, DALEY THOMPSON* and *ALLAN WELLS,* for their dedication and total commitment under severe pressure . . . and a whole queue of golfers headed by the one and only *JACK NICKLAUS.* I admire their professionalism and conduct on and off the course.

DILIP VENGSARKAR *(Bombay and India)*
BJORN BORG, who proved on courts throughout the world that he was the greatest of lawn tennis champions. He played with great skill and concentration and never let his emotions get the better of him.

BILL VOCE *(Nottinghamshire and England)*
BJORN BORG. I admire his general attitude, his determination and his calmness. He was an outstanding champion, particularly at Wimbledon where at his peak he was unbeatable.

PETER WALKER *(Glamorgan and England)*
LYNN DAVIES, the former Olympic, European and

Commonwealth long jump champion from Wales. He overcame the dual handicap of lack of opportunity and geographical isolation to emerge as a supreme competitor in his field.

DOUG WALTERS *(New South Wales and Australia)*
JOHN NEWCOMBE, a great player and a great sportsman who has been a credit to lawn tennis and Australia wherever he has played. His record at Wimbledon proves that he was one of the masters of his sport.

JOHNNY WARDLE *(Yorkshire and England)*
STANLEY MATTHEWS. He was a gentleman as well as being a footballing genius. The way he accepted all the knocks on the field and the disappointments on the occasions when he was left out of the England team was a lesson to all. He had a genuine love for his sport and he spread this totally involved feeling to the spectators.

WASIM BARI *(Pakistan International Airways and Pakistan)*
JEHANGHIR KHAN, the world squash champion who has lifted the standards of his sport to new heights. He is totally dedicated and supremely fit. His reflexes, range of wristy shots and speed around the court are quite remarkable.

ALLAN WATKINS *(Glamorgan and England)*
Golfer **LEE TREVINO,** a great personality and entertainer who underneath all the banter and fun is a marvellous competitor with an awful lot of ability.

BOB WILLIS *(Surrey, Warwickshire and England)*
MUHAMMAD ALI. He was exceptional at his sport and entertained at the same time as revealing his great talent. I don't think many people realise just how fit one has to be to become a world boxing champion. I liked him for his style and also his humour.

DON WILSON *(Yorkshire and England)*
JACK NICKLAUS, not only a great professional and master of his game but also a wonderful sportsman on and off the course.

BOB WOOLMER *(Kent and England)*
There are many sportsmen that I admire but I suppose the number one has to be *STEVE OVETT* for his single-minded dedication to winning.

NORMAN YARDLEY *(Yorkshire and England)*
JACK NICKLAUS, a model for anyone reaching the top in their sport. He is, of course, a magnificent golfer but more than that, he gives pleasure and entertainment with his pleasant manner.

SECTION SIX
AROUND THE GROUNDS

Seventy-five Test cricketers name their favourite grounds

DENNIS AMISS *(Warwickshire and England)*
WORCESTER, for its beautiful picture-postcard setting and its good, true, fast wicket.

GEOFF ARNOLD *(Surrey, Sussex and England)*
I select *OLD TRAFFORD* because the crowds there are always encouraging with their support and I like the wicket. It is green and assists the seamers.

TREVOR BAILEY *(Essex and England)*
CHALKWELL PARK, a pretty, compact ground in West-cliff-on-Sea, Essex. Not only does the ground hold many fond memories for me but it just happens to be the closest one to my home.

ALEC BEDSER *(Surrey and England)*
I must choose *LORD'S.* It is a ground soaked in tradition and atmosphere and there is an air of discipline about the place that inspires cricketers to produce their best.

GEOFFREY BOYCOTT *(Yorkshire and England)*
I judge a ground by the feeling I get the moment I walk into it. I can always quickly pick up the atmosphere and know whether it's right for me. The grounds to which I have taken an instant liking are at Adelaide, Sydney, Antigua, Barbados and Trinidad.

MIKE BREARLEY *(Middlesex and England)*
It has to be *LORD'S,* despite the ridge! I have scores of
happy memories of leading Middlesex and England teams
out on to that historic ground.

DAVID BROWN *(Warwickshire and England)*
For me, it just has to be *LORD'S*. You can 'feel' the
tradition and the atmosphere of the place. Everything
about it is just right.

TOM CARTWRIGHT *(Warwickshire, Somerset, Glamorgan and England)*
LORD'S . . . because I always found it exciting to play
there. It has a unique atmosphere and a wicket that is kind
to medium-pace bowlers.

BRIAN CLOSE *(Yorkshire, Somerset and England)*
I have happy memories of many Yorkshire grounds but
the ones I particularly liked were those in Somerset. They
were small, compact and you felt you had a special contact
with the spectators.

DENIS COMPTON *(Middlesex and England)*
LORD'S, naturally, is my number one choice but I have
three others very close to my heart for a variety of reasons
– *OLD TRAFFORD, TRENT BRIDGE* and *THE OVAL.*

MIKE DENNESS *(Kent, Essex and England)*
THE MOAT ground at Maidstone, Kent, not only because
I almost always managed to score runs there but because it
is compact and picturesque.

TED DEXTER *(Sussex and England)*
I liked *OLD TRAFFORD* best of all. It's a good 'seeing'
ground for batsmen and there's always a nice, warm
Lancashire welcome for visitors.

BILL EDRICH *(Middlesex and England)*
LORD'S – my second home! I have so many wonderful

memories of playing there, particularly scoring 1,000 runs there before the end of May in 1938.

JOHN EDRICH *(Surrey and England)*
TRENT BRIDGE, because I usually managed to get runs there. *LORD'S, SYDNEY* and *HEADINGLEY* are close behind and I particularly loved the Yorkshire crowds. They were knowledgeable and hospitable.

GODFREY EVANS *(Kent and England)*
LORD'S for atmosphere . . . *NEWLANDS* in Cape Town for a beautiful, picturesque setting.

KEITH FLETCHER *(Essex and England)*
LORD'S, particularly on the fourth day of a Test match when the wicket has become absolutely flat. There's no ground quite like Lord's for atmosphere.

MIKE GATTING *(Middlesex and England)*
LORD'S. It continually brings the best out of individual players and teams and is also one of the best-equipped grounds in the world.

SUNIL GAVASKAR *(Bombay, Somerset and India)*
QUEEN'S PARK OVAL in Trinidad. It is a beautiful ground with a lovely backdrop.

GRAHAM GOOCH *(Essex and England)*
WORCESTER and CHELMSFORD . . . because the playing surfaces at both grounds are very good and there is a nice 'feel' and atmosphere to each place. They are not surrounded by cold concrete and stands.

DAVID GOWER *(Leicestershire and England)*
SYDNEY. It does not have as much history or bureaucracy as Lord's but plenty of atmosphere. And it's definitely warmer! I would consider it almost perfect if I could score a century there. Incidentally, it's just as difficult to get past the gatemen as at Lord's!

TOM GRAVENEY *(Gloucestershire, Worcestershire and England)*
WORCESTER, the perfect County ground. LORDS'S, THE OVAL and TRENT BRIDGE for the big-match occasion.

KIM HUGHES *(Western Australia and Australia)*
MELBOURNE CRICKET GROUND when there's a big crowd. The noise and involvement of the spectators makes every game memorable.

SIR LEN HUTTON *(Yorkshire and England)*
BRADFORD PARK AVENUE was the ground where I always felt at home. I was made welcome by my 'own folk' and the ground was small enough to encourage you to go for your shots. There was an excellent sight screen and I always fancied my chances of hitting sixes there.

RAY ILLINGWORTH *(Yorkshire, Leicester and England)*
For purely personal reasons, I like the **DOVER** ground but for the really special, spine-tingling atmosphere you can't beat **LORD'S** on the first day of an England–Australia Test.

IMRAN KHAN *(Lahore, Oxford University, Worcs, Sussex, and Pakistan)*
MELBOURNE CRICKET GROUND, partly because of the excitement generated by the usually huge crowds and also because of a wicket that used to be excellent, although it has recently deteriorated somewhat.

DOUG INSOLE *(Essex and England)*
THE ADELAIDE OVAL tops my list because of it's scenic beauty. Not far behind come **LORD'S** and **NEWLANDS** in Cape Town. All are marvellous grounds in their own exclusive way.

ROBIN JACKMAN *(Surrey and England)*
NEWLANDS in Cape Town. It is quite the most picturesque first-class ground on which I have played.

SYED KIRMANI *(Mysore and India)*
EDEN GARDENS, Calcutta. It is a huge ground with rarely less than 100,000 spectators packed in for Test matches. Anybody performing well there is a hero. The atmosphere can bring the best out of players.

ALAN KNOTT *(Kent and England)*
SYDNEY CRICKET GROUND. It's large, pretty, has the famous Hill and there are excellent training, practice and changing facilities for the players.

JIM LAKER *(Surrey, Essex and England)*
KENNINGTON OVAL, the scene of so many triumphs in the 1950s. I have warm memories of the place.

DAVID LARTER *(Northamptonshire and England)*
LORD'S. Nowhere else has the atmosphere and it's a good bowling wicket.

JOHN LEVER *(Essex and England)*
ILFORD CRICKET CLUB ground at Valentine's Park where I played as a club cricketer and made my County debut. The Ilford wicket usually helps the quick bowlers.

TONY LEWIS *(Glamorgan and England)*
LORD'S. You get a great feeling of occasions just being there. From a personal point of view it was also one of my lucky grounds where I made several centuries, including for Cambridge against Oxford University, for MCC against Yorkshire and for Glamorgan against Somerset.

DENNIS LILLEE *(Western Australia and Australia)*
MELBOURNE CRICKET GROUND holds a lot of happy memories for me. I always enjoy playing there and had my best return of 13 for 22 on that wicket and managed to

take 11 wickets in the Centenary Test there against England in 1977.

DAVID LLOYD *(Lancashire and England)*
I like the peaceful, picturesque grounds at **CANTER-BURY, CHESTERFIELD and TUNBRIDGE WELLS** but have also enjoyed the big-match occasions at **TRENT BRIDGE, OLD TRAFFORD and THE OVAL** which are needed commercially.

BRIAN LUCKHURST *(Kent and England)*
CANTERBURY. Most cricketers are superstitious and Canterbury was one of my 'lucky' grounds where I usually managed to score runs. It is also one of the loveliest of all the grounds.

RODNEY MARSH *(Western Australia and Australia)*
SYDNEY CRICKET GROUND. It's got everything: it's the right size, has perfect facilities and generally a good cricket wicket.

PETER MAY *(Surrey and England)*
KENNINGTON OVAL, scene of so many memorable Surrey triumphs during the 1950s.

COLIN MILBURN *(Northamptonshire and England)*
It has to be **LORD'S.** There is no place to match it for atmosphere when it is full and the greatest thrill of my life was to score a century there against the West Indies in 1966.

ARTHUR MILTON *(Gloucestershire and England)*
TRENT BRIDGE. It has a wonderful turf and there is a sense of history about the pavilion that is in direct line with the wicket.

ARTHUR McINTYRE *(Surrey and England)*
TRENT BRIDGE. The wicket, the outfield, the sight

screen, the dressing-room and amenities – all were just right.

JOHN MURRAY *(Middlesex and England)*
LORD'S, where I spent the happiest 25 years of my life and made so many lovely friends.

ALAN OAKMAN *(Sussex and England)*
HOVE. I learned all my cricket there and spent many happy days in the sun and used to think how nice and relaxing it was for members to be able to sit in deckchairs watching the cricket.

JIM PARKS *(Sussex, Somerset and England)*
HOVE. I have so many happy memories of playing on what I considered a 'lucky' and beautifully situated ground.

PAT POCOCK *(Surrey and England)*
The *UNIVERSITY GROUND* in Sri Lanka – for the atmosphere and breath-taking scenic beauty.

JOHN PRICE *(Middlesex and England)*
Where else but *LORD'S?* I was lucky enough to play most of my cricket there and can't believe there are many better grounds. At a lower level, the *SIDMOUTH* Cricket Club ground in Devonshire is a very pleasant venue.

PETER RICHARDSON *(Worcestershire, Kent and England)*
OLD TRAFFORD. I always felt at home there and usually managed to score runs.

BRIAN ROSE *(Somerset and England)*
TAUNTON, which has retained its rural atmosphere even though now graced with a new pavilion. It is small and compact with a lovely outfield and a good wicket.

191

DEREK SHACKLETON *(Hampshire and England)*
LORD'S, mainly because it suited my style of bowling. I was particularly happy bowling from the nursery end where I had the slight slope to help me.

PHIL SHARPE *(Yorkshire, Derbyshire and England)*
SCARBOROUGH, BRAMALL LANE and *EDGBASTON* for batting . . . *HULL, BRAMALL LANE* and *BRADFORD* for catching . . . *THE PARKS, WORCESTER, CANTERBURY, BOURNEMOUTH, TRINIDAD* and *VANCOUVER* for scenery.

REG SIMPSON *(Nottinghamshire and England)*
My home town ground, *TRENT BRIDGE*. It is not too large but compact with an excellent outfield and square. It is a very good 'seeing' ground for batsmen and there is always a special atmosphere about the place.

ALAN SMITH *(Warwickshire and England)*
LORD'S because of its unique atmosphere. You can sense the history the moment you walk into the ground.

MIKE SMITH *(Leicestershire, Warwickshire and England)*
LORD'S, for all its atmosphere and great tradition. It was always an honour to play there.

JOHN SNOW *(Sussex, Warwickshire and England)*
SYDNEY because of the success I enjoyed there and *LORD'S* for its history and atmosphere.

BRIAN STATHAM *(Lancashire and England)*
OLD TRAFFORD for atmosphere, seeing the ball and an affinity with the crowd. The prettiest ground is *NEWLANDS* at Cape Town, with an avenue of oaks on one side and Table Mountain as a backdrop on the other side. Quite breath-taking.

DICK SPOONER *(Warwickshire and England)*
LORD'S. I always enjoyed playing there for the atmosphere alone. There is no place quite like it.

DAVID STEELE *(Northamptonshire, Derbyshire and England)*
TRENT BRIDGE. Apart from the fact that it is an excellent ground, I have a special regard for it because of my Test century there.

RAY TATTERSALL *(Lancashire and England)*
LORD'S, for its great atmosphere, appreciative, neutral crowd, facilities and a wicket that helped both batsmen and bowlers. I also like the food that was served!

BOB TAYLOR *(Derbyshire and England)*
SYDNEY, for its big-occasion atmosphere, particularly in Test matches when you can 'feel' the tension in the air. I particularly enjoyed playing night cricket there.

FRED TITMUS *(Middlesex, Surrey and England)*
LORD'S, of course. Is there any other ground? There is no place to match it for atmosphere, tradition, facilities and just about everything. It revives so many happy cricketing memories for me.

ROGER TOLCHARD *(Leicestershire and England)*
COCKINGTON at Torquay. It's a big, 'U' shape and sets problems like no other place.

FRED TRUEMAN *(Yorkshire, Derbyshire and England)*
LORD'S, which has everything: history, atmosphere and a wicket on which it was a joy to bowl.

DEREK UNDERWOOD *(Kent and England)*
SYDNEY CRICKET GROUND, not least because I shall never forget us regaining the Ashes there in 1971. I like the unique atmosphere of the place and the surroundings.

DILIP VENGSARKAR *(Bombay and India)*
BRABOURNE STADIUM in Bombay has got the best atmosphere as far as major-occasion matches go. The crowd generates a feeling of great excitement and anticipation.

BILL VOCE *(Nottinghamshire and England)*
TRENT BRIDGE because it was a very good sporting wicket that was true but fast. It gave the bowlers as well as the batsmen a chance.

PETER WALKER *(Glamorgan and England)*
LORD'S, for the sheer sense of awe and historical atmosphere. It is quite unique. No other ground in the world reeks of tradition in quite the same way.

DOUG WALTERS *(New South Wales and Australia)*
SYDNEY CRICKET GROUND. It has atmosphere and the crowd appreciate what they are watching and are quick to acknowledge good cricket whether it be by the home side or the visitors.

JOHNNY WARDLE *(Yorkshire and England)*
OLD TRAFFORD. The wicket was always immaculate, the light was better than at any other Test ground and it was an excellent strip when dry but took spin after rain.

WASIM BARI *(Pakistan International Airways and Pakistan)*
ADELAIDE OVAL. It has excellent facilities for the players and the surroundings are quite beautiful. It is always a pleasure to play there.

ALLAN WATKINS *(Glamorgan and England)*
SWANSEA, for its wonderful atmosphere and friendly and knowledgeable crowd.

PETER WILLEY *(Northamptonshire and England)*
I can't be pinned down to naming one ground. I consider any ground marvellous if I score runs there. For instance, I was very fond of *THE OVAL* after my first century there in Test cricket. I judge each ground by my form on the day.

BOB WILLIS *(Surrey, Warwickshire and England)*
LORD'S, which even when empty has the most atmosphere of any ground in the world.

DON WILSON *(Yorkshire and England)*
LORD'S, the Mecca of the game. Even now that I'm working at the ground every day as coach, it is still a thrill for me every time I walk through the gates.

BOB WOOLMER *(Kent and England)*
LORD'S, the headquarters of cricket with all its great history and tradition. I had the wonderful experience of making my Test debut at Lord's against Australia in 1975 and in the same year took a hat-trick there against the Aussies.

DOUG WRIGHT *(Kent and England)*
CANTERBURY, a peaceful, picturesque ground and to play there was always a pleasure.

SECTION SEVEN
FOR ARGUMENT'S SAKE

General team lists compiled by the Editor

ALL-STAR STAR-SIGN TEAMS
(Restricted to post-war Test players)

CAPRICORN
(21 December–19 January)

Hanif Mohammad *(Pakistan)*
21.12.34
Arthur Morris *(Australia)*
19.1.22
Clyde Walcott *(West Indies)*
17.1.26
Peter May *(England)*
31.1.19
Colin Cowdrey *(England)*
24.12.32
Doug Walters *(Australia)*
21.12.45
John Waite *(South Africa)*+
19.1.30
Kapil Dev *(India)*
6.1.59
Johnny Wardle *(England)*
8.1.23
Ian Meckiff *(Australia)*
6.1.35
Wayne Daniel *(West Indies)*
16.1.56
12th man:
Nawab of Pataudi Jnr *(India)*

AQUARIUS
(20 January–19 February)

Bill Lawry *(Australia)*
11.2.37
Brian Luckhurst *(England)*
5.2.39
Kim Hughes *(Australia)*
26.1.54
Gundappa Viswanath *(India)*
12.2.49
Bev Congdon *(New Zealand)*
11.2.38
Peter Walker *(England)*
17.2.36
Don Tallon *(Australia)*+
17.2.16
Jim Laker *(England)*
9.2.32
Freddie Trueman *(England)*
6.2.31
Andy Roberts *(West Indies)*
29.1.51
Michael Holding *(West Indies)*
16.2.54
12th man:
Fazal Mahmood *(India)*

+ *Wicket-keeper*

PISCES
(19 Feb–20 Mar)

David Sheppard *(England)*
6.3.29
Nari Contractor *(India)*
7.3.34
Viv Richards *(West Indies)*
7.3.52
Graeme Pollock *(South Africa)*
27.2.44
Everton Weekes *(West Indies)*
26.2.25
Brian Close *(England)*
24.2.31
Farokh Engineer *(India)*+
25.2.38
Phil Edmonds *(England)*
8.3.58
Bill Johnston *(Australia)*
26.2.22
John Lever *(England)*
4.3.49
Rodney Hogg *(Australia)*
5.3.51
12th man:
Graham Dowling *(New Zealand)*
4.3.37

ARIES
(21 Mar–20 Apl)

Glenn Turner *(New Zealand)*
26.5.47
Dennis Amiss *(England)*
7.4.43
David Gower *(England)*
1.4.57
Bill Edrich *(England)*
26.3.16
Alvin Kallicharran *(West Indies)*
21.3.49
Colin Bland *(South Africa)*
5.4.38
Vinoo Mankad *(India)*
12.4.17
Alan Knott *(England)*+
9.4.46
Norman Gifford *(England)*
30.3.40
Malcolm Marshall *(West Indies)*
18.4.58
Norman Cowans *(England)*
17.4.61
12th man:
Jeff Stollmeyer *(West Indies)*
11.4.21

TAURUS
(21 April–20 May)

Mike Brearley *(England)*
28.4.42
Gordon Greenidge *(West Indies)*
1.5.51
Conrad Hunte *(West Indies)*
9.5.32
Keith Fletcher *(England)*
20.5.44
Ted Dexter *(England)*
15.5.35
Javed Burki *(Pakistan)*
8.5.38
Deryck Murray *(West Indies)+*
20.5.43
Graham Dilley *(England)*
18.5.59
Sonny Ramadhin *(West Indies)*
1.5.30
Alf Valentine *(West Indies)*
29.4.30
David Larter *(England)*
24.4.40
12th man:
Ian Redpath *(Australia)*
11.5.41

GEMINI
(21 May–21 June)

John Edrich *(England)*
21.6.37
Tom Graveney *(England)*
16.6.27
David Murray *(West Indies)*
29.5.50
Denis Compton *(England)*
23.5.18
Wally Hammond *(England)*
19.6.03
Alan Davidson *(Australia)*
14.6.29
Ray Illingworth *(England)*
8.6.32
Bob Willis *(England)*
30.5.49
Frank Tyson *(England)*
6.6.30
Brian Statham *(England)*
16.6.30
Derek Underwood *(England)*
8.6.45
12th man:
Javed Miandad *(Pakistan)*
12.6.57

CANCER
(22 June–21 July)

Sunil Gavaskar *(India)*
10.7.49
Len Hutton *(England)*
23.6.16
Barry Richards *(South Africa)*
21.7.45
Mike Smith *(England)*
30.6.33
Garfield Sobers *(West Indies)*
18.7.36
Richard Hadlee *(New Zealand)*
3.7.51
Bob Taylor *(England)*+
17.4.41
Tony Lock *(England)*
5.7.29
Graham McKenzie *(Australia)*
24.6.41
Dennis Lillee *(Australia)*
18.7.49
Alec Bedser *(England)*
4.7.18
12th man:
Peter Pollock *(South Africa)*
30.6.41

LEO
(22 July–21 August)

Graham Gooch *(England)*
23.7.53
Trevor Goddard *(South Africa)*
1.8.31
Zaheer Abbas *(Pakistan)*
24.7.47
Greg Chappell *(Australia)*
7.8.48
Frank Worrell *(West Indies)*
1.8.24
Godfrey Evans *(England)*+
18.8.20
John Emburey *(England)*
20.8.52
Jeff Thomson *(Australia)*
16.8.50
Derek Shackleton *(England)*
12.8.24
Tom Cartwright *(England)*
22.7.35
Roy Tattersall *(England)*
17.8.22
12th man:
Alan Turner *(Australia)*
23.7.50

VIRGO
(22 August–21 September)

Kepler Wessels *(Australia)*
14.9.57
Lindsay Hassett *(Australia)*
28.8.13
Don Bradman *(Australia)*
27.8.08
Basil Butcher *(West Indies)*
3.9.33
Clive Lloyd *(West Indies)*
31.8.44
Mike Procter *(South Africa)*
15.9.46
Gil Langley *(Australia)*+
19.9.19
Max Walker *(Australia)*
12.9.48
Geoff Miller *(England)*
8.9.52
Wes Hall *(West Indies)*
12.9.37
Geoff Arnold *(England)*
3.9.44
12th man:
Bruce Yardley *(Australia*
7.9.47

LIBRA
(22 September–22 October)

Geoff Boycott *(England)*
21.10.40
Bob Barber *(England)*
26.9.35
Ian Chappell *(Australia)*
26.9.43
Neil Harvey *(Australia)*
8.10.28
Mohinder Amarnarth *(India)*
24.9.50
Basil D'Oliveira *(England)*
4.10.31
Jim Parks *(England)*+
21.10.31
Richie Benaud *(Australia)*
6.10.21
Ray Lindwall *(Australia)*
3.10.21
John Snow *(England)*
13.10.41
Bishen Bedi *(India)*
25.9.46
12th man:
Keith Boyce *(West Indies)*
11.10.43

SCORPIO
(23 October–21 November)

Colin Milburn *(England)*
23.10.41
Chris Tavaré *(England)*
27.10.54
Roy Fredericks *(West Indies)*
11.11.42
Colin McDonald *(Australia)*
17.11.28
Bruce Laird *(Australia)*
21.11.50
Ken MacKay *(Australia)*
24.10.25
Rodney Marsh *(Australia)*+
4.11.47
Peter Loader *(England)*
25.10.29
David Allen *England*
29.10.29
Bruce Dooland *(Australia)*
1.11.23
Alan Moss *(England)*
14.11.30
12th man:
Jack Birkenshaw *(England)*
13.11.40

SAGITTARIUS
(22 November–20 December)

Cyril Washbrook *(England)*
6.12.41
Mike Denness *(England)*
1.12.40
Ken Barrington *(England)*
24.11.30
Imran Khan *(Pakistan)*
25.11.52
Ian Botham *(England)*
24.11.55
Trevor Bailey *(England)*
3.12.23
Keith Miller *(Australia)*
28.11.19
Fred Titmus *(England)*
24.11.32
Keith Andrew *(England)*+
15.12.29
Joel Garner *(West Indies)*
16.12.52
Charlie Griffith *(West Indies)*
14.12.38
12th man:
Rick McCosker *(Australia)*
11.12.46

A TEAM OF LEFT-HANDERS

John Edrich *(England)*
Bill Lawry *(Australia)*
Graeme Pollock *(South Africa)*
Neil Harvey *(Australia)*
Frank Woolley *(England)*
Garfield Sobers *(West Indies)*
Phil Mead *(England)*
George Brown *(England)*+
Alan Davidson *(Australia)*
Hedley Verity *(England)*
Bill Johnston *(Australia)*
12th man:
Derek Underwood *(England)*

THE BESPECTACLED BRIGADE

Geoff Boycott *(England)*
Roy Marshall *(West Indies)*
Zaheer Abbas *(Pakistan)*
Eddie Barlow *(South Africa)*
Mike Smith *(England)*
Clive Lloyd *(West Indies)*
David Steele *(England)*
Dick Young *(England)*+
Tufty Mann *(South Africa)*
Alf Valentine *(West Indies)*
Bill Bowes *(England)*
12th man:
Walter Hadlee *(New Zealand)*

FOREIGN-BORN ENGLAND TEST PLAYERS

Bob Woolmer *(Kent)*
Kanpur, India 15.5.48
Chris Smith *(Hampshire)*
Durban, South Africa
15.10.58
Colin Cowdrey *(Kent)*
Bangalore, India 24.21.32
Ted Dexter *(Sussex)*
Milan, Italy 15.5.35
Basil D'Oliveira
(Worcestershire)
Cape Town, South Africa
4.10.31
Freddie Brown *(Surrey & Northants)*
Lima, Peru 16.12.10
Tony Greig *(Sussex)*
Queenstown, South Africa
6.10.46
Derek Pringle *(Essex)*
Nairobi, Kenya 18.9.58
Phil Edmonds *(Middlesex)*
Lusaka, Zambia 8.3.51
Gubby Allen *(Middlesex)*
Sydney, Australia 13.7.02
Robin Jackman *(Surrey)*
Simla, India 13.8.45
12th man:
Roland Butcher *(Middlesex)*
Barbados, West Indies
14.10.53

CRICKETING FOOTBALLERS

Arthur Milton
(Gloucestershire)
Arsenal left winger
Bill Edrich *(Middlesex)*
Tottenham winger
Phil Neale *(Worcestershire)*
Lincoln City full-back
Denis Compton *(Middlesex)*
Arsenal left winger
Willie Watson *(Yorks & Leics)*
Sunderland inside forward
Ken Taylor *(Yorkshire)*
Huddersfield half-back
Chris Balderstone *(Leics)*
Huddersfield & Carlisle
forward
Brian Close
(Yorkshire & Somerset)
Bradford City inside forward
Leslie Compton *(Middlesex)*+
Arsenal centre-half
David Smith *(Gloucestershire)*
Bristol City & Millwall
forward
Jim Standen *(Worcestershire)*
West Ham goalkeeper
12th man:
Ian Botham *(Somerset)*
Scunthorpe all-rounder

A TEAM OF ALL-ROUNDERS

Eddie Barlow *(South Africa)*
Farokh Engineer *(India)+*
Mike Procter *(South Africa)*
Garfield Sobers *(West Indies)*
Ian Botham *(England)*
Imran Khan *(Pakistan)*
Keith Miller *(Australia)*
Alan Davidson *(Australia)*
Richard Hadlee *(New Zealand)*
Kapil Dev *(India)*
Richie Benaud *(Australia)*
12th man:
Frank Worrell *(West Indies)*

COMMENTATING CRICKETERS

Bob Simpson *(Australia)*
Colin Milburn *(England)*
Ted Dexter *(England)*
Tony Lewis *(England)*
Tom Graveney *(England)+*
Tony Greig *(England)*
Trevor Bailey *(England)*
Richie Benaud *(Australia)*
Jim Laker *(England)*
Fred Trueman *(England)*
Frank Tyson *(England)*
12th man:
Peter Walker *(England)*

COUNTY SELECT

(Restricted to post-war County players. In a case where a cricketer has represented more than one County he has been considered for only one team)

DERBYSHIRE

Eddie Barlow
John Wright
Peter Kirsten
Lawrence Rowe
Donald Carr *(capt)*
Geoff Miller
Bob Taylor+
Mike Hendrick
Les Jackson
Cliff Gladwin
Michael Holding
12th man:
Alan Ward

ESSEX

Graham Gooch
Gordon Barker
Ken McEwan
Keith Fletcher *(capt)*
Doug Insole
Trevor Bailey
Keith Boyce
Neil Foster
Brian Taylor+
Ray East
John Lever
12th man:
Barry Knight

GLAMORGAN

Gilbert Parkhouse
Alan Jones
Majid Khan
Tony Lewis *(capt)*
Javed Miandad
Peter Walker
Allan Watkins
Tom Cartwright
Don Shepherd
Eifion Jones+
Jeff Jones
12th man:
Jim McConnon

GLOUCESTERSHIRE

Sadiq Mohammad
George Emmett
Zaheer Abbas
Wally Hammond *(capt)*
Arthur Milton
Mike Procter
David Shepherd
John Mortimore
Roy Swetman+
David Allen
David Smith
12th man:
Tony Brown

HAMPSHIRE

Barry Richards
Gordon Greenidge
Roy Marshall
Colin Ingleby-McKenzie *(capt)*
Trevor Jesty
Leo Harrison+
Malcolm Marshall
Peter Sainsbury
Andy Roberts
Derek Shackleton
Bob Cottam
12th man:
Chris Smith

KENT

Brian Luckhurst
Chris Tavaré
Bob Woolmer
Colin Cowdrey *(capt)*
Mike Denness
Asif Iqbal
Alan Knott
Godfrey Evans+
Graham Dilley
Doug Wright
Derek Underwood
12th man:
John Shepherd

LANCASHIRE

Cyril Washbrook *(capt)*
Geoff Pullar
Graeme Fowler
Clive Lloyd
David Lloyd
Barry Wood
Jack Ikin
Farokh Engineer+
Roy Tattersall
Brian Statham
Peter Lever
12th man:
Frank Hayes

LEICESTERSHIRE

Willie Watson
Chris Balderstone
David Gower
Brian Davison
Charles Palmer
Roger Tolchard+
Ray Illingworth *(capt)*
Nick Cook
Ken Shuttleworth
Ken Higgs
Graham McKenzie
12th man:
Jack Birkenshaw

MIDDLESEX

Mike Brearley *(capt)*
Jack Robertson
Bill Edrich
Denis Compton
Mike Gatting
Peter Parfitt
Phil Edmonds
John Murray+
Fred Titmus
Wayne Daniel
Alan Moss
12th man:
John Emburey

NORTHAMPTONSHIRE

Colin Milburn
Wayne Larkins
David Steele
Mushtaq Mohammad
Peter Willey
Dennis Brookes *(capt)*
George Tribe
Keith Andrew+
Sarfraz Nawaz
Frank Tyson
Bishen Bedi
12th man:
Freddie Brown

NOTTINGHAMSHIRE

Reg Simpson *(capt)*
Brian Bolus
Derek Randall
Clive Rice
Garfield Sobers
Basharat Hassan
Richard Hadlee
Bruce Dooland
Eddie Hemmings
Geoff Millman+
Harold Butler
12th man:
Ken Smales

SOMERSET

Harold Gimblett
Brian Rose
Viv Richards
Bill Alley
Colin McCool
Ian Botham
Maurice Tremlett *(capt)*
Vic Marks
Harold Stephenson+
Joel Garner
Fred Rumsey
12th man:
Ken Palmer

SURREY

John Edrich
Mickey Stewart
Peter May *(capt)*
Ken Barrington
Geoff Howarth
Arthur McIntyre+
Jim Laker
Tony Lock
Sylvester Clarke
Peter Loader
Alec Bedser
12th man:
Graham Roope

WARWICKSHIRE

Dennis Amiss
Bob Barber
Rohan Kanhai
Alvin Kallicharran
Mike Smith *(capt)*
Tom Dollery
Deryck Murray+
David Brown
Bob Willis
Eric Hollies
Lance Gibbs
12th man:
John Jameson

SUSSEX

David Sheppard
Ken Suttle
Ted Dexter *(capt)*
Nawab of Pataudi, jnr
Tony Greig
Imran Khan
Alan Oakman
Jim Parks+
Ian Thomson
John Snow
Geoff Arnold
12th man:
Paul Parker

WORCESTERSHIRE

Glenn Turner
Don Kenyon
Peter Richardson
Tom Graveney *(capt)*
Basil D'Oliveira
Martin Horton
Reg Perks
Brian Booth+
Norman Gifford
Les Flavell
Vanburn Holder
12th man:
Roley Jenkins

YORKSHIRE

Len Hutton *(capt)*
Geoff Boycott
Phil Sharpe
John Hampshire
Brian Close
Doug Padgett
Jimmy Binks+
Johnny Wardle
Chris Old
Fred Trueman
Bob Appleyard
12th man:
Norman Yardley

A TEAM OF POST-WAR TEST CAPTAINS

Len Hutton *(England)*
Sunil Gavaskar *(India)*
Peter May *(England)*
Greg Chappell *(Australia)*
Clive Lloyd *(West Indies)*
Trevor Goddard *(South Africa)*
John Reid *(New Zealand)* +
Imran Khan *(Pakistan)*
Richie Benaud *(Australia)*
Bob Willis *(England)*
Bishen Bedi *(India)*
12th man:
Mike Brearley *(England)*

INTERNATIONAL POST-WAR ALL-STARS

Hanif Mohammad *(Pakistan)*
Mike Denness *(Scotland)*
Barry Richards *(South Africa)*
Duleep Mendis *(Sri Lanka)*
Tony Lewis *(Wales)*
Clyde Walcott *(West Indies)* +
Ian Botham *(England)*
Vinoo Mankad *(India)*
Duncan Fletcher *(Zimbabwe)*
Richard Hadlee *(New Zealand)*
Dennis Lillee *(Australia)*
12th man:
Ollie Mortensen *(Holland)*

ERNIE WISE'S
DREAM TEAM

1 **LEN HUTTON**
2 **GEOFF BOYCOTT**
3 **TOM GRAVENEY**
4 **DENIS COMPTON**
5 **IAN BOTHAM**
6 **TREVOR BAILEY**
7 **GODFREY EVANS+**
8 **JOHNNY WARDLE**
9 **JIM LAKER**
10 **FREDDIE TRUEMAN**
11 **BOB WILLIS**

'You'll notice that there's a lot of Yorkshire grit and class running through the team. Openers Hutton and Boycott would give the team just the right foundation and then Botham, Compton and Graveney could build on it with their flashing strokes. If there is any danger of a collapse it would quickly be halted by "Barnacle" Bailey. Freddie Trueman and Bob Willis would be magnificent new ball partners, supported by the swing of Botham and Bailey. Then Laker and Wardle can provide their special brand of spin magic and behind the stumps there's the one and only Godfrey Evans, the greatest of all wicket-keepers. I don't think there's a single weakness in the team.'

ERNIE WISE

ERNIE WISE, who was the short half of the brilliant Morecambe and Wise comedy duo and famous for the plays 'what he wrote,' has been a cricket follower ever since his formative years in his native Yorkshire where his personal favourite was the great Len Hutton.

DREAM MATCH 1:
FATHERS v SONS

FATHERS XI

Len Hutton
James Parks
George Headley
Nawab of Pataudi
Colin Cowdrey
Walter Hadlee
Joe Hardstaff+
Vinoo Mankad
Jahangir Khan
Dave Nourse
Fred Tate
12th man:
Datta Gaekwad

SONS XI

Majid Khan
Jim Parks+
Joe Hardstaff
Nawab of Pataudi
Ron Headley
Chris Cowdrey
Dudley Nourse
Ashok Mankad
Richard Hutton
Richard Hadlee
Maurice Tate
12th man:
Anshuman Gaekwad

DREAM MATCH 2:
OLDER BROTHERS v YOUNGER BROTHERS

OLDER BROTHERS XI

Eric Rowan *(1909)*
Peter Richardson *(1931)*
Ian Chappell *(1943)*
Surinder Amarnath *(1948)*
Eric Bedser *(1918)*
Wazir Mohammad *(1929)*
Richie Benaud *(1930)*
Leslie Compton *(1912)*+
Peter Pollock *(1941)*
Dayle Hadlee *(1948)*
Fergie Gupte *(1929)*
12th man:
Denis Atkinson *(1926)*

YOUNGER BROTHERS XI

Hanif Mohammad *(1934)*
Mohinder Amarnath *(1950)*
Graeme Pollock *(1944)*+
Denis Compton *(1918)*
Greg Chappell *(1948)*
John Benaud *(1944)*
Dick Richardson *(1934)*
Athol Rowan *(1921)*
Richard Hadlee *(1951)*
Alec Bedser *(1918)*
Baloo Gupte *(1934)*
12th man:
Eric Atkinson *(1927)*

NB: Graeme Pollock is makeshift wicket-keeper for the young brothers. His father was a first-rate 'keeper and so he has a good pedigree. Alec Bedser was born just a matter of minutes after his twin brother Eric.

DREAM MATCH 3:
WORLD PRE-WAR v WORLD POST-WAR

PRE-WAR XI (1918–40)

Jack Hobbs *(England)*
Herbert Sutcliffe *(England)*
Don Bradman *(Australia)*
Walter Hammond *(England)*
George Headley *(West Indies)*
Frank Woolley *(England)*
Learie Constantine *(West Indies)*
Bert Oldfield *(Australia)*+
Jack Gregory *(Australia)*
Harold Larwood *(England)*
Hedley Verity *(England)*
12th man:
Maurice Tate *(England)*

POST-WAR XI

Len Hutton *(England)*
Sunil Gavaskar *(India)*
Viv Richards *(West Indies)*
Peter May *(England)*
Denis Compton *(England)*
Garry Sobers *(West Indies)*
Ian Botham *(England)*
Richie Benaud *(Australia)*
Ray Lindwall *(Australia)*
Rodney Marsh *(Australia)*+
Dennis Lillee *(Australia)*
12th man:
Barry Richards *(South Africa)*

DREAM MATCH 4:
ENGLAND v REST OF THE WORLD

(No players from Dream Match 3 were considered)

POST-WAR ENGLAND XI

Geoff Boycott *(Yorkshire)*
John Edrich *(Surrey)*
Colin Cowdrey *(Kent)*
Ken Barrington *(Surrey)*
Tom Graveney *(Glos & Worcs)*
Trevor Bailey *(Essex)*
Alan Knott *(Kent)*+
Jim Laker *(Surrey)*
Fred Trueman *(Yorkshire)*
Alec Bedser *(Surrey)*
Derek Underwood *(Kent)*
12th man:

REST OF THE WORLD XI

Hanif Mohammad *(Pakistan)*
Trevor Goddard *(South Africa)*
Graeme Pollock *(South Africa)*
Neil Harvey *(Australia)*
Greg Chappell *(Australia)*
Farokh Engineer *(India)*+
Keith Miller *(Australia)*
Imran Khan *(Pakistan)*
Michael Holding *(West Indies)*
Bishen Bedi *(India)*
Lance Gibbs *(West Indies)*
12th man:

TIM RICE'S
DREAM TEAM

1 **LEN HUTTON** *(capt)*
2 **BILL EDRICH**
3 **PETER MAY**
4 **DENIS COMPTON**
5 **TOM GRAVENEY**
6 **TREVOR BAILEY**
7 **GODFREY EVANS+**
8 **JIM LAKER**
9 **TONY LOCK**
10 **FRED TRUEMAN**
11 **ALEC BEDSER**

'This is the team that won the Ashes in 1953 and was the first game of first-class cricket I followed as it happened on radio and television (not every ball as these days, but towards the end of the match I remember the BBC cancelling other radio programmes to continue the commentary). This XI has always remained my 'dream team' and every single member of the side would hold his own in any world XI. I only wish that could be said of some of the England teams of recent times.'

TIM RICE

TIM RICE, who has put the words to Andrew Lloyd-Webber's music in such smash-hit shows as *Jesus Christ Superstar* and *Evita*, always waxes lyrical on the subject of cricket, which is his first love. He is a keen weekend cricketer who admits that his top 'dream team' includes him as opening batsman and opening bowler in an England side that beats Australia by an innings and 500 runs!

SECTION EIGHT
TOP TEN TABLES

Statistical facts and figures compiled by Malcolm
Rowley
(including all Test matches up to 6 January 1984)

THE BATTING MASTERS

Top Ten Test scorers, with their Test career span in brackets

ALL-TIME LIST

		Tests	Inns	Runs	Avge
1	**Sunil Gavaskar** *(1970–)*	99	174	8394	52.46
2	**Geoff Boycott** *(1965–82)*	108	193	8114	47.72
3	**Garfield Sobers** *(1953–74)*	93	160	8032	57.78
4	**Colin Cowdrey** *(1954–75)*	114	188	7624	44.06
5	**Walter Hammond** *(1927–47)*	85	140	7249	58.45
6	**Greg Chappell** *(1970–84)*	87	151	7110	53.86
7	**Don Bradman** *(1928–48)*	52	80	6996	99.94
8	**Len Hutton** *(1937–55)*	79	138	6971	56.67
9	**Ken Barrington** *(1955–68)*	82	131	6806	58.67
10	**Clive Lloyd** *(1966–)*	96	157	6734	46.44

For ENGLAND

		Tests	Inns	Runs	Avge
1	**Geoff Boycott** *(1965–82)*	108	193	8114	47.72
2	**Colin Cowdrey** *(1954–75)*	114	188	7624	44.06
3	**Walter Hammond** *(1927–47)*	85	140	7249	58.45
4	**Len Hutton** *(1937–55)*	79	138	6971	56.67
5	**Ken Barrington** *(1955–68)*	82	131	6806	58.67
6	**Denis Compton** *(1937–57)*	78	131	5807	50.06
7	**Jack Hobbs** *(1907–30)*	61	102	5401	56.94
8	**John Edrich** *(1963–76)*	77	127	5138	43.54
9	**Tom Graveney** *(1951–69)*	79	123	4882	44.38
10	**Herbert Sutcliffe** *(1924–35)*	54	84	4555	60.73

For AUSTRALIA

	Tests	Inns	Runs	Avge
1 Greg Chappell *(1970–84)*	87	151	7110	53.86
2 Don Bradman *(1928–48)*	52	80	6996	99.94
3 Neil Harvey *(1947–63)*	79	137	6149	48.41
4 Doug Walters *(1965–81)*	74	125	5357	48.26
5 Ian Chappell *(1964–80)*	75	136	5345	42.42
6 Bill Lawry *(1961–71)*	67	123	5234	47.15
7 Bobby Simpson *(1957–78)*	62	111	4869	46.81
8 Ian Redpath *(1963–76)*	66	120	4737	43.45
9 Kim Hughes *(1977–)*	61	106	4119	41.19
10 Allan Border *(1978–)*	56	97	3968	49.60

For SOUTH AFRICA

	Tests	Inns	Runs	Avge
1 Bruce Mitchell *(1929–49)*	42	80	3471	48.88
2 Dudley Nourse *(1935–51)*	34	62	2960	53.81
3 Herbie Taylor *(1912–32)*	42	76	2936	40.77
4 Eddie Barlow *(1961–70)*	30	57	2516	45.74
5 Trevor Goddard *(1955–70)*	41	78	2516	34.46
6 Jackie McGlew *(1951–62)*	34	64	2440	42.06
7 John Waite *(1951–65)*	50	86	2405	30.44
8 Graeme Pollock *(1963–70)*	23	41	2256	60.97
9 Dave Nourse *(1902–24)*	45	83	2234	29.78
10 Roy McLean *(1951–65)*	40	73	2120	30.28

For WEST INDIES

	Tests	Inns	Runs	Avge
1 Garfield Sobers *(1953–74)*	93	160	8032	57.78
2 Clive Lloyd *(1966–)*	96	157	6734	46.44
3 Rohan Kanhai *(1957–74)*	79	137	6227	47.53
4 Everton Weekes *(1947–58)*	48	81	4455	58.61
5 Viv Richards *(1974–)*	56	89	4717	55.49
6 Alvin Kallicharran *(1971–80)*	66	109	4399	44.43
7 Roy Fredericks *(1968–77)*	59	109	4344	42.49
8 Frank Worrell *(1947–63)*	51	87	3860	49.48
9 Clyde Walcott *(1947–60)*	44	74	3798	56.68
10 Gordon Greenidge *(1974–)*	47	80	3373	46.20

For NEW ZEALAND

	Tests	Inns	Runs	Avge
1 **Bev Congdon** *(1964–78)*	61	114	3448	32.22
2 **John Reid** *(1949–65)*	58	108	3428	33.28
3 **Glenn Turner** *(1968–)*	41	73	2991	44.64
4 **Bert Sutcliffe** *(1946–65)*	42	76	2727	40.10
5 **Mark Burgess** *(1967–78)*	50	92	2684	31.20
6 **Graham Dowling** *(1961–72)*	39	77	2306	31.16
7 **Geoff Howarth** *(1974–)*	34	62	2014	35.33
8 **Richard Hadlee** *(1972–)*	44	77	1601	24.25
9 **Brian Hastings** *(1968–76)*	31	56	1510	30.20
10 **John Parker** *(1972–79)*	36	63	1498	24.55

For INDIA

	Tests	Inns	Runs	Avge
1 **Sunil Gavaskar** *(1970–)*	99	174	8394	52.46
2 **Gundappa Viswanath** *(1969–)*	91	155	6080	41.93
3 **Dilip Vengsarkar** *(1975–)*	69	113	3970	38.54
4 **Polly Umrigar** *(1948–62)*	59	94	3631	42.22
5 **Vijay Manjrekar** *(1951–65)*	55	92	3208	39.12
6 **Chandra Borde** *(1958–70)*	55	97	3061	35.59
7 **Nawab of Pataudi** *(1961–75)*	46	83	2792	34.90
8 **Mohinder Amarnath** *(1969–)*	42	72	2670	39.85
9 **Farokh Engineer** *(1961–75)*	46	87	2611	31.08
10 **Kapil Dev** *(1978–)*	62	92	2483	29.55

For PAKISTAN

	Tests	Inns	Runs	Avge
1 **Zaheer Abbas** *(1969–)*	66	106	4552	46.44
2 **Javed Miandad** *(1976–)*	60	95	4519	55.79
3 **Majid Khan** *(1964–83)*	63	106	3931	38.92
4 **Hanif Mohammad** *(1952–70)*	55	97	3915	43.98
5 **Mushtaq Mohammad** *(1958–79)*	57	100	3643	39.17
6 **Asif Iqbal** *(1964–79)*	58	99	3575	38.85
7 **Saeed Ahmed** *(1957–73)*	41	78	2991	40.41
8 **Sadiq Mohammad** **(1969–80)**	41	74	2579	35.81
9 **Wasim Raja** *(1972–)*	50	80	2546	37.44
10 **Mudassar Nazar** *(1976–)*	43	66	2526	41.40

THE BOWLING KINGS

Top Ten Test bowlers, with their Test career span in brackets

ALL-TIME LIST

	Tests	Balls	Wkts	Avge
1 Dennis Lillee *(1970–84)*	70	18467	355	23.92
2 Lance Gibbs *(1957–76)*	79	27115	309	29.09
3 Fred Trueman *(1952–65)*	67	15178	307	21.57
4 Bob Willis *(1970–)*	83	16045	305	24.49
5 Derek Underwood *(1966–82)*	86	21860	297	24.49
6 Ian Botham *(1977–)*	63	14727	277	24.82
7 Bishen Bedi *(1966–79)*	67	21364	266	28.71
8 Brian Statham *(1950–65)*	70	16056	252	24.84
9 Richie Benaud *(1951–64)*	63	19108	248	27.03
10 Kapil Dev *(1978–)*	62	13342	247	27.70

For ENGLAND

	Tests	Balls	Wkts	Avge
1 Fred Trueman *(1952–65)*	67	15178	307	21.57
2 Bob Willis *(1970–)*	83	16045	305	24.49
3 Derek Underwood *(1966–82)*	86	21860	297	25.83
4 Ian Botham *(1977–)*	63	14727	277	24.82
5 Brian Statham *(1950–65)*	70	16056	252	24.84
6 Alec Bedser *(1946–55)*	51	15918	236	24.89
7 John Snow *(1965–76)*	49	12021	202	26.66
8 Jim Laker *(1947–59)*	46	12027	193	21.24
9 Sidney Barnes *(1901–14)*	27	7873	189	16.43
10 Tony Lock *(1952–68)*	49	13147	174	25.58

For AUSTRALIA

	Tests	Balls	Wkts	Avge
1 **Dennis Lillee** *(1970–84)*	70	18467	355	23.92
2 **Richie Benaud** *(1951–64)*	63	19108	248	27.03
3 **Graham MacKenzie** *(1961–71)*	60	17681	246	29.78
4 **Ray Lindwall** *(1945–60)*	61	13650	228	23.03
5 **Clarrie Grimmett** *(1924–36)*	37	14153	216	24.21
6 **Jeff Thomson** *(1972–)*	49	10205	197	27.03
7 **Alan Davidson** *(1952–63)*	44	11587	186	20.53
8 **Keith Miller** *(1945–57)*	55	10461	170	22.97
9 **Bill Johnston** *(1947–55)*	40	11048	160	23.91
10 **Bill O'Reilly** *(1931–46)*	27	10024	144	22.59

For SOUTH AFRICA

	Tests	Balls	Wkts	Avge
1 **Hugh Tayfield** *(1949–60)*	37	13568	170	25.91
2 **Trevor Goddard** *(1955–70)*	41	11735	123	26.22
3 **Peter Pollock** *(1961–70)*	28	6522	116	24.18
4 **Neil Adcock** *(1953–62)*	26	6391	104	21.10
5 **Cyril Vincent** *(1927–35)*	25	5863	84	31.32
6 **Aubrey Faulkner** *1905–24)*	25	4321	82	26.58
7 **Bert Vogler** *(1905–11)*	15	2764	64	22.73
8 **Jimmy Sinclair** *(1895–1911)*	25	3598	63	31.68
9 **Jimmy Blanckenberg** *(1913–24)*	18	3888	60	30.28
10 **Peter Heine** *(1955–62)*	14	3890	58	25.08

For WEST INDIES

	Tests	Balls	Wkts	Avge
1 **Lance Gibbs** *(1957–76)*	79	27115	309	29.09
2 **Garfield Sobers** *(1953–74)*	93	21599	235	34.03
3 **Andy Roberts** *(1973–)*	47	11127	202	25.61
4 **Wes Hall** *(1958–69)*	48	10421	192	26.38
5 **Michael Holding** *(1975–)*	42	9477	181	24.07
6 **Sonny Ramadhin** *(1950–61)*	43	13939	158	28.98
7 **Alf Valentine** *(1950–62)*	36	12961	139	30.32
8 **Joel Garner** *(1976–)*	32	7326	131	21.83
9 **Colin Croft** *(1976–81)*	27	6165	125	23.30
10 **Vanburn Holder** *(1969–79)*	40	9095	109	33.27

For NEW ZEALAND

		Tests	Balls	Wkts	Avge
1	Richard Hadlee *(1972–)*	44	11355	200	25.82
2	Richard Collinge *(1964–78)*	35	7689	116	29.25
3	Bruce Taylor *(1964–73)*	30	6334	111	26.60
4	Dick Motz (1961–69)	32	7034	100	31.48
5	Lance Cairns *(1973–)*	32	8005	97	31.91
6	Hedley Howarth *(1969–77)*	30	8833	86	36.95
7	John Reid *(1949–65)*	58	7725	85	33.35
8	Dayle Hadlee *(1969–77)*	26	4883	71	33.64
9	Tony MacGibbon *(1950–58)*	26	5659	70	30.85
10	Francis Cameron *(1961–65)*	19	4570	61	30.31

For INDIA

		Tests	Balls	Wkts	Avge
1	Bishen Bedi *(1966–79)*	67	21364	266	28.71
2	Kapil Dev *(1978–)*	62	13342	247	27.70
3	Chandrasekhar *(1963–79)*	58	15963	242	29.74
4	Erapally Prasanna *(1961–79)*	49	14353	189	30.38
5	Vinoo Mankad *(1946–59)*	44	14686	162	32.32
6	Venkataraghavan *(1964–83)*	57	14877	156	36.11
7	Fergie Gupte *(1951–62)*	36	11284	149	29.54
8	Dilip Doshi *(1979–)*	33	9320	114	30.72
9	Karsan Ghavri *(1974–81)*	39	7042	109	33.54
10	Bapu Nadkarni *(1955–68)*	41	9175	88	29.06

For PAKISTAN

		Tests	Balls	Wkts	Avge
1	Imran Khan *(1971–)*	51	12552	232	22.92
2	Sarfraz Nawaz *(1968–)*	52	12379	163	33.36
3	Fazal Mahmood *(1952–62)*	34	9834	139	24.70
4	Intikhab Alam *(1959–77)*	47	10474	125	35.95
5	Iqbal Qasim *(1976–)*	37	9372	115	29.94
6	Mushtaq Mohammad *(1958–79)*	57	5410	79	29.24
7	Abdul Qadir *(1977–)*	24	6320	88	38.05
8	Mahmood Hussain *(1952–62)*	27	5976	68	38.64
9	Sikander Bakht *(1976–)*	26	4870	67	35.98
10	Pervez Sajjad *(1964–73)*	19	4145	59	23.89

NICHOLAS PARSONS'
DREAM TEAM

1 JACK HOBBS
2 SUNIL GAVASKAR
3 DON BRADMAN
4 DENIS COMPTON
5 VIV RICHARDS
6 GARFIELD SOBERS
7 IAN BOTHAM
8 GODFREY EVANS
9 RAY LINDWALL
10 JIM LAKER
11 FRED TRUEMAN

'I found this team selection extremely difficult. How can one possibly pick a team from all the players – both those you have seen and other legendary figures you have read and heard about – when so many giants have trod the 'cricket stage' of our national game? I am embarrassed at having to omit such great players as Len Hutton, Greg Chappell, Barry Richards, Keith Miller, Derek Underwood and so many more. In the end I have gone for a balanced side, with players who could not only blend as a team but who could individually unleash that excitement and great flair that is so much a part of the great game of cricket.'

NICHOLAS PARSONS

NICHOLAS PARSONS, the man with all the answers on Sale of the Century and a versatile comedy actor, is a keen Lord's Taverner and so devoted to the game that he once produced and directed a film called Mad Dogs and Cricketers. His secret ambition in life has always been to open the innings for England against Australia at Lord's and to read in the headlines the next day: PARSONS SCORES A WHALE OF A CENTURY . . .!

TOP INDIVIDUAL TEST SCORES

365* **Garfield Sobers**
West Indies v. Pakistan Kingston 1958

364 **Len Hutton**
England v. Australia The Oval 1938

337 **Hanif Mohammad**
Pakistan v. West Indies Bridgetown 1958

336* **Walter Hammond**
England v. New Zealand Auckland 1933

334† **Don Bradman**
Australia v. England Headingley 1930

325 **Andrew Sandham**
England v. West Indies Kingston 1930

311 **Bobby Simpson**
Australia v. England Old Trafford 1964

310* **John Edrich**
England v. New Zealand Headingley 1965

307 **Bob Cowper**
Australia v. England Melbourne 1966

302 **Lawrence Rowe**
West Indies v. England Bridgetown 1974

TOP WICKET-TAKERS IN A TEST MATCH INNINGS

10–53†† **Jim Laker**
England v. Australia Old Trafford 1956

9–28 **George Lohman**
England v. South Africa Johannesburg 1896

9–69 **Jasubhai Patel**
India v. Australia Kanpur 1959

9–83 **Kapil Dev**
India v. West Indies Ahmedabad 1983

9–86 **Sarfraz Nawaz**
Pakistan v. Australia Melbourne 1979

9–95 **Jack Noreiga**
West Indies v. India Port of Spain 1971

9–102 **Subhash Gupte**
India v. West Indies Kanpur 1958

9–103 **Sydney Barnes**
England v. South Africa Johannesburg 1913

9–113 **Hugh Tayfield**
South Africa v. England Johannesburg 1957

9–121 **Arthur Mailey**
Australia v. England Melbourne 1921

---

* Not out
† Don Bradman also scored 304 v. England at Headingley in 1934
†† Jim Laker also took 9–37 v. Australia in the 1956 Old Trafford Test

TOP TEN TEST WICKET-KEEPERS

		Tests	Dsmls	Ct	Avge
1	**Rodney Marsh** *(1970–　)*	96	355	343	12
2	**Alan Knott** *(1967–81)*	95	269	250	19
3	**Wasim Bari** *(1967–　)*	81	228	201	27
4	**Godfrey Evans** *(1946–59)*	91	219	173	46
5	**Deryck Murray** *(1963–80)*	62	189	181	8
6	**Wally Grout** *(1957–66)*	51	187	163	24
7	**Syed Kirmani** *(1975–　)*	78	179	145	34
8	**Bob Taylor** *(1970–　)*	51	162	155	7
9	**John Waite** *(1951–65)*	50	141	124	17
10	**Bert Oldfield** *(1920–37)*	54	130	78	52

TOP TEN TEST CATCHERS
(not including wicket-keepers)

		Tests	Catches
1	**Greg Chappell** *(1970–84)*	87	122
2	**Colin Cowdrey** *(1954–75)*	114	120
3	**Bobby Simpson** *(1957–78)*	62	110
4	**Walter Hammond** *(1927–47)*	85	110
5	**Garfield Sobers** *(1953–74)*	93	109
6	**Ian Chappell** *(1964–80)*	75	105
7	**Tony Greig** *(1972–77)*	58	87
8	**Sunil Gavaskar** *(1970–　)*	99	85
9	**Ian Redpath** *(1963–76)*	66	83
10	**Tom Graveney** *(1951–69)*	79	80

TOP TEN CAREER AGGREGATES (Batting)

Batsmen who scored the majority of their runs in post-war, English first-class cricket (career span in brackets)

		Runs	Inns	N.O.	Top	Avge
1	Tom Graveney *(1948–72)*	47793	1223	159	258	44.91
2	Geoff Boycott *(1962–)*	44210	925	139	261*	56.24
3	Len Hutton *(1934–60)*	40140	814	91	364	55.51
4	Mike Smith *(1951–75)*	39832	1091	139	204	44.84
5	John Edrich *(1956–78)*	39790	979	104	310*	45.47
6	Denis Compton *(1936–64)*	38942	839	88	300	51.85
7	Don Kenyon *(1946–67)*	37002	1159	59	259	33.63
8	Bill Edrich *(1934–58)*	36965	964	92	267*	42.39
9	Dennis Amiss *(1960–)*	36879	954	102	262*	43.28
10	Jim Parks *(1949–76)*	36673	1227	172	205*	34.76

* Not out

TOP TEN CAREER AGGREGATES (Bowling)

Bowlers who took the majority of their wickets in post-war, English first-class cricket

		Wkts	Runs	Avge
1	Derek Shackleton *(1948–69)*	2857	53303	18.65
2	Tony Lock *(1946–71)*	2844	54701	19.23
3	Fred Titmus *(1949–82)*	2830	63313	22.37
4	Eric Hollies *(1932–57)*	2323	48656	20.94
5	Fred Trueman *(1949–69)*	2304	42154	18.29
6	Brian Statham *(1950–68)*	2260	36995	16.36
7	Derek Underwood *(1963–)*	2224	44014	19.79
8	Don Shepherd *(1950–72)*	2218	47298	21.32
9	Trevor Bailey *(1945–67)*	2082	48170	23.13
10	Ray Illingworth *(1951–83)*	2072	42023	20.28

All Futura Books are available at your bookshop or newsagent, or can be ordered from the following address:
Futura Books, Cash Sales Department,
P.O. Box 11, Falmouth, Cornwall

Please send cheque or postal order (no currency), and allow 55p for postage and packing for the first book plus 22p for the second book and 14p for each additional book ordered up to a maximum charge of £1.75 in U.K.

Customers in Eire and B.F.P.O. please allow 55p for the first book, 22p for the second book plus 14p per copy for the next 7 books, thereafter 8p per book.

Overseas customers please allow £1.00 for postage and packing for the first book and 25p per copy for each additional book.